365 DAILY DEVOTIONS

5 Minutes a DAY

Real Questions...Real Answers

Her Devotional

TO

_____

FROM

_____

DATE

_____

365 DAILY DEVOTIONS

5 Minutes a DAY

Real Questions...Real Answers

Her Devotional

INTRODUCTION

Can you spare a few minutes each day for God? Of course you can . . . and of course you should! No matter how busy you are, you should never allow the temptations and distractions of everyday living to distance you from your Creator.

Being a young woman in today's world isn't easy. This world offers limitless opportunities to stray from the path that God intends for your life. You are confronted with temptations and distractions that were unknown to previous generations. And, the world is changing so rapidly that, at times, it seems difficult to catch your breath and keep your balance. This book is intended to help.

This book contains 365 devotional readings of particular interest to young women like you. The chapters contain Bible verses, brief devotional readings, and quotations from noted Christian women and men.

Do you have questions that you can't answer? Are you seeking to change some aspect of your life? Do you desire the eternal abundance and peace that can be yours through Christ? If so, ask for God's help and ask for it many times each day . . . starting with a regular, heartfelt morning devotional. Even a few minutes is enough time to change your day . . . and your life.

THIS IS THE DAY

This is the day the Lord has made; we will rejoice and be glad in it.

Psalm 118:24 NKJV

Are you basically a thankful person? Do you appreciate the stuff you've got and the life that you're privileged to live? You most certainly should be thankful. After all, when you stop to think about it, God has given you more blessings than you can count. So the question of the day is this: will you slow down long enough to thank your Heavenly Father . . . or not?

Sometimes, life here on earth can be complicated, demanding, and frustrating. When the demands of life leave you rushing from place to place with scarcely a moment to spare, you may fail to pause and thank your Creator for the countless blessings He has given you. Failing to thank God is understandable . . . but it's wrong.

God's Word makes it clear: a wise heart is a thankful heart. Period. Your Heavenly Father has blessed you beyond measure, and you owe Him everything, including your thanks. God is always listening—are you willing to say thanks? It's up to you, and the next move is yours.

USING GOD'S GIFTS

Based on the gift they have received, everyone should use it to serve others, as good managers of the varied grace of God.

1 Peter 4:10 Holman CSB

The gifts that you possess are gifts from the Giver of all things good. Do you have a spiritual gift? Share it. Do you have a testimony about the things that Christ has done for you? Don't leave your story untold. Do you posses financial resources? Share them. Do you have particular talents? Hone your skills and use them for God's glory.

When you hoard the treasures that God has given you, you live in rebellion against His commandments. But, when you obey God by sharing His gifts freely and without fanfare, you invite Him to bless you more and more. Today, be a faithful steward of your talents and treasures. And then prepare yourself for even greater blessings that are sure to come.

—.—.—.—.—.—.—

When God crowns our merits, he is crowning nothing other than his gifts.

St. Augustine

JUMPSTARTING YOUR DAY

Therefore, get your minds ready for action, being self-disciplined, and set your hope completely on the grace to be brought to you at the revelation of Jesus Christ.

1 Peter 1:13 Holman CSB

Are you willing to spend a few minutes every day with God? And are you willing to jumpstart your day by spending a few quiet moments studying God's Word, or are you too busy for that? The answer, of course, is that you can find time for God . . . and you should.

Scottish-born evangelist Henry Drummond correctly observed, "Ten minutes spent in Christ's company every day—even two minutes—will make the whole day different." How true. If you dedicate even a few minutes each morning to a time of devotional reading and prayer, you will change the tone and direction of your day.

Are you seeking to change some aspect of your life? Do you seek to improve the condition of your spiritual or physical health? Do you desire the peace that can be yours through Christ? If so, ask for God's help and ask for it many times each day . . . starting with a regular morning download of God's wisdom, God's truth, and God's love.

YOUR PARTNERSHIP WITH GOD

For it is God who is working among you both the willing and the working for His good purpose.

Philippians 2:13 Holman CSB

Do you seek a life of purpose, abundance, and fulfillment? If so, then you must form a partnership with God.

You are God's work-in-progress. God wants to mold your heart and guide your path, but because He created you as a creature of free will, He will not force you to become His. That choice is yours alone, and it is a choice that should be reflected in every decision you make and every step you take.

Today, as you encounter the challenges of everyday life, strengthen your partnership with God through prayer, through obedience, through praise, through thanksgiving, and through service. God is the ultimate partner, and He wants to be your partner in every aspect of your life. Please don't turn Him down.

—.—.—.—.—.—.—.—

No matter what we are going through, no matter how long the waiting for answers, of one thing we may be sure. God is faithful. He keeps His promises. What he starts, He finishes . . . including His perfect work in us.

Gloria Gaither

GUARD YOUR THOUGHTS

Blessed are the pure in heart, because they will see God.

Matthew 5:8 Holman CSB

What is your focus today? Are you willing to focus your thoughts on the countless blessings that God has given you? Before you answer that question, consider this: the direction of your thoughts will determine, to a surprising extent, the direction of your day and your life.

This day—and every day hereafter—is a chance to celebrate the life that God has given you. It's a chance to celebrate your relationships, your talents, and your opportunities. So focus your thoughts upon the gift of life—and upon the blessings that surround you.

You're a beautiful creation of God, a being of infinite importance. Give thanks for your gifts and share them. Never have the needs—or the opportunities for service—been greater.

—.—.—.—.—.—

The things we think are the things that feed our souls. If we think on pure and lovely things, we shall grow pure and lovely like them; and the converse is equally true.

Hannah Whitall Smith

A POWER BEYOND UNDERSTANDING

I pray also that you will have greater understanding in your heart so you will know the hope to which he has called us and that you will know how rich and glorious are the blessings God has promised his holy people. And you will know that God's power is very great for us who believe.

Ephesians 1:18-19 NCV

Ours is a God of infinite possibilities. But sometimes, because of limited faith and limited understanding, we wrongly assume that God cannot or will not intervene in the affairs of mankind. Such assumptions are simply wrong.

Are you afraid to ask God to do big things in your life? Is your faith threadbare and worn? If so, it's time to abandon your doubts and reclaim your faith in God's promises.

God's Word makes it clear: absolutely nothing is impossible for the Lord. And since the Bible means what it says, you can be comforted in the knowledge that the Creator of the universe can do miraculous things in your own life and in the lives of your loved ones. Your challenge, as a believer, is to take God at His word, and to expect the miraculous.

FINISHING THE WORK

A patient spirit is better than a proud spirit.

Ecclesiastes 7:8 Holman CSB

As you continue to seek God's purpose for your life, you will undoubtedly experience your fair share of disappointments, detours, false starts, and failures. When you do, don't become discouraged: God's not finished with you yet.

The old saying is as true today as it was when it was first spoken: "Life is a marathon, not a sprint." That's why wise travelers select a traveling companion who never tires and never falters. That partner, of course, is your Heavenly Father.

Are you tired? Ask God for strength. Are you discouraged? Believe in His promises. Are you defeated? Pray as if everything depended upon God, and work as if everything depended upon you. And finally, have faith that you play important role in God's great plan for mankind—because you do.

—.—.—.—.—.—

Your life is not a boring stretch of highway. It's a straight line to heaven. And just look at the fields ripening along the way. Look at the tenacity and endurance. Look at the grains of righteousness. You'll have quite a crop at harvest . . . so don't give up!

Joni Eareckson Tada

FEARS IN PERSPECTIVE

They won't be afraid of bad news; their hearts are steady because they trust the Lord.

Psalm 112:7 NCV

His adoring fans called him the "Sultan of Swat." He was Babe Ruth, the baseball player who set records for home runs and strikeouts. Babe's philosophy was simple. He said, "Never let the fear of striking out get in your way." That's smart advice on the diamond or off.

Of course it's never wise to take foolish risks (so buckle up, slow down, and don't do anything silly). But when it comes to the game of life, you should not let the fear of failure keep you from taking your swings.

Today, ask God for the courage to step beyond the boundaries of your self-doubts. Ask Him to guide you to a place where you can realize your full potential—a place where you are freed from the fear of failure. Ask Him to do His part, and promise Him that you will do your part. Don't ask Him to lead you to a "safe" place; ask Him to lead you to the "right" place . . . and remember: those two places are seldom the same.

—.—.—.—.—.—.—

God shields us from most of the things we fear, but when He chooses not to shield us, He unfailingly allots grace in the measure needed.

Elisabeth Elliot

TAPPING INTO GOD'S STRENGTH

For the eyes of the Lord are on the righteous and his ears are attentive to their prayer, but the Lord is against those who do evil.

1 Peter 3:12 NIV

Have you made God the cornerstone of your life, or is He relegated to a few hours on Sunday morning? Have you genuinely allowed God to reign over every corner of your heart, or have you attempted to place Him in a spiritual compartment? The answer to these questions will determine the direction of your day and your life.

God loves you. In times of trouble, He will comfort you; in times of sorrow, He will dry your tears. When you are weak or sorrowful, God is as near as your next breath. He stands at the door of your heart and waits. Welcome Him in and allow Him to rule. And then, accept the peace, the strength, the protection, and the abundance that only God can give.

—.—.—.—.—.—.—

When all else is gone, God is left, and nothing changes Him.

Hannah Whitall Smith

WHY AM I HERE?

May He grant you according to your heart's desire, and fulfill all your purpose.

Psalm 20:4 NKJV

"Why did God put me here?" It's an easy question to ask and, at times, a very difficult question to answer. As you seek to answer that question, God's purposes will not always be clear to you. Sometimes you may wander aimlessly in a wilderness of your own making. And sometimes, you may struggle mightily against God in a vain effort to find success and happiness through your own means, not His.

Are you earnestly seeking to discern God's purpose for your life? If so, these pages are intended as a reminder of several important facts: 1. God has a plan for your life; 2. If you seek that plan sincerely and prayerfully, you will find it; 3. When you discover God's purpose for your life, you will experience abundance, peace, joy, and power—God's power. And that's the only kind of power that really matters.

—.—.—.—.—.—.—

The Creator has made us each one of a kind. There is nobody else exactly like us, and there never will be. Each of us is his special creation and is alive for a distinctive purpose.

Luci Swindoll

TRUST HIM

Trust the Lord with all your heart, and don't depend on your own understanding. Remember the Lord in all you do, and he will give you success.

Proverbs 3:5-6 NCV

Sometimes the future seems bright, and sometimes it does not. Yet even when we cannot see the possibilities of tomorrow, God can. As believers, our challenge is to trust an uncertain future to an all-powerful God.

When we trust God, we should trust Him without reservation. We should steel ourselves against the inevitable disappointments of the day, secure in the knowledge that our Heavenly Father has a plan for the future that only He can see.

Can you place your future into the hands of a loving and all-knowing God? Can you live amid the uncertainties of today, knowing that God has dominion over all your tomorrows? If you can, you are wise and you are blessed. When you trust God with everything you are and everything you have, He will bless you now and forever.

—.—.—.—.—.—.—

Never be afraid to trust an unknown future to a known God.

Corrie ten Boom

FAITH ABOVE FEELINGS

Now the just shall live by faith.

Hebrews 10:38 NKJV

Hebrews 10:38 teaches that we should live by faith. Yet sometimes, despite our best intentions, negative feelings can rob us of the peace and abundance that would otherwise be ours through Christ. When anger or anxiety separates us from the spiritual blessings that God has in store, we must rethink our priorities and renew our faith. And we must place faith above feelings. Human emotions are highly variable, decidedly unpredictable, and often unreliable. Our emotions are like the weather, only far more fickle. So we must learn to live by faith, not by the ups and downs of our own emotional roller coasters.

Sometime during this day, you will probably be gripped by a strong negative emotion. Distrust it. Reign it in. Test it. And turn it over to God. Your emotions will inevitably change; God will not. So trust Him completely as you watch your feelings slowly evaporate into thin air—which, of course, they will.

—.—.—.—.—.—.—

We are to live by faith, not feelings.

Kay Arthur

BEYOND ENVY

We can't afford to waste a minute, must not squander these precious daylight hours in frivolity and indulgence, in sleeping around and dissipation, in bickering and grabbing everything in sight. Get out of bed and get dressed! Don't loiter and linger, waiting until the very last minute. Dress yourselves in Christ, and be up and about!

Romans 13:13-14 MSG

Because we are frail, imperfect human beings, we are sometimes envious of others. But God's Word warns us that envy is sin. Thus, we must guard ourselves against the natural tendency to feel resentment and jealousy when other people experience good fortune.

As believers, we have absolutely no reason to be envious of any people on earth. After all, as Christians we are already recipients of the greatest gift in all creation: God's grace. We have been promised the gift of eternal life through God's only begotten Son, and we must count that gift as our most precious possession.

Rather than giving in to the sin of envy, we should focus on the marvelous things that God has done for us—starting with Christ's sacrifice. And we must refrain from preoccupying ourselves with the blessings that God has chosen to give others.

PREPARING FOR LIFE . . . AND DEATH

Alive, I'm Christ's messenger; dead, I'm his bounty. Life versus even more life! I can't lose.

Philippians 1:21 MSG

God has given you the gift of life. How will you use that gift? Will you allow God's Son to reign over your heart? And will you treat each day as a precious treasure from your Heavenly Father? You should, and, hopefully, you will.

Every day that we live, we should be preparing to die. If we seek to live purposeful, productive lives, we will be ever mindful that our time here on earth is limited, and we will conduct ourselves accordingly.

Life is a glorious opportunity, but it is also shockingly brief. We must serve God each day as if it were our last day. When we do, we prepare ourselves for the inevitable end of life here on earth, and or the victory that is certain to follow.

—.—.—.—.—.—.—

We are not meant to die merely in order to be dead. God could not want that for the creatures to whom He has given the breath of life. We die in order to live.

Elisabeth Elliot

ENTHUSIASM FOR LIFE AND FOR WORK

Do your work with enthusiasm. Work as if you were serving the Lord, not as if you were serving only men and women.

Ephesians 6:7 NCV

Do you see each day as a glorious opportunity to serve God and to do His will? Are you enthused about life, or do you struggle through each day giving scarcely a thought to God's blessings? Are you constantly praising God for His gifts, and are you sharing His Good News with the world? And are you excited about the possibilities for service that God has placed before you, whether at home, at work, at church, or at school? You should be.

You are the recipient of Christ's sacrificial love. Accept it enthusiastically and share it fervently. Jesus deserves your enthusiasm; the world deserves it; and you deserve the experience of sharing it.

—.—.—.—.—.—.—

Enthusiasm, like the flu, is contagious—we get it from one another.

Barbara Johnson

BODY CARE

Don't you know that you are God's temple and that God's Spirit lives in you?

1 Corinthians 3:16 NCV

How do you treat your body? Do you treat it with the reverence and respect it deserves, or do you take it more or less for granted? Well, the Bible has clear instructions about the way you should take care of the miraculous body that God has given you.

God's Word teaches us that our bodies are "temples" that belong to God (1 Corinthians 6:19-20). We are commanded (not encouraged, not advised—we are commanded!) to treat our bodies with respect and honor. We do so by making wise choices and by making those choices consistently over an extended period of time.

Do you sincerely seek to improve the overall quality of your life and your health? Then promise yourself—and God—that you will begin making the kind of wise choices that will lead to a longer, healthier, happier life. The responsibility for those choices is yours. And so are the rewards.

—.—.—.—.—.—.—.—

Those whose hearts are pure are the temples of the Holy Spirit.

Luci Swindoll

ENTRUSTING OUR HOPES TO GOD

You, Lord, give true peace to those who depend on you, because they trust you.

Isaiah 26:3 NCV

The hope that the world offers is fleeting and imperfect. The hope that God offers is unchanging, unshakable, and unending. It is no wonder, then, that when we seek security from worldly sources, our hopes are often dashed. Thankfully, God has no such record of failure.

Where will you place your hopes today? Will you entrust your future to man or to God? Will you seek solace exclusively from fallible human beings, or will you place your hopes, first and foremost, in the trusting hands of your Creator? The decision is yours, and you must live with the results of the choice you make.

For thoughtful believers, hope begins with God. Period. So today, as you embark upon the next stage of your life's journey, consider the words of the Psalmist: "You are my hope; O Lord GOD, You are my confidence" (71:5 NASB). Then, place your trust in the One who cannot be shaken.

—.—.—.—.—.—.—.—

Faith is the belief that God will do what is right.

Max Lucado

TRUSTING GOD'S LOVE

For I am persuaded that neither death nor life, nor angels nor rulers, nor things present, nor things to come, nor powers, nor height, nor depth, nor any other created thing will have the power to separate us from the love of God that is in Christ Jesus our Lord!

Romans 8:38-39 Holman CSB

The Bible makes it clear: God's got a plan—a very big plan—and you're an important part of that plan. But here's the catch: God won't force His plans upon you; you've got to figure things out for yourself . . . or not.

As a follower of Christ, you should ask yourself this question: "How closely can I make my plans match God's plans?" The more closely you manage to follow the path that God intends for your life, the better.

Do you have questions or concerns about the future? Take them to God in prayer. Do you have hopes and expectations? Talk to God about your dreams. Are you carefully planning for the days and weeks ahead? Consult God as you establish your priorities. Turn every concern over to your Heavenly Father, and sincerely seek His guidance—prayerfully, earnestly, and often. Then, listen for His answers . . . and trust the answers that He gives.

CONCERNING THE LOVE OF MONEY

Keep your lives free from the love of money, and be satisfied with what you have.

Hebrews 13:5 NCV

In our modern society, we need money to live. But as Christians, we must never make the acquisition of money the central focus of our lives. Money is a tool, but it should never overwhelm our sensibilities. The focus of life must be squarely on things spiritual, not things material.

Whenever we place our love for material possessions above our love for God—or when we yield to the countless other temptations of everyday living—we find ourselves engaged in a struggle between good and evil, a clash between God and Satan. Our responses to these struggles have implications that echo throughout our families and throughout our communities. Let us choose wisely by freeing ourselves from that subtle yet powerful temptation: the temptation to love the world more than we love God.

—.—.—.—.—.—.—.—

When we put people before possessions in our hearts, we are sowing seeds of enduring satisfaction.

Beverly LaHaye

WHATEVER IT IS, GOD IS BIGGER

Jesus turned around and said to her, "Daughter, be encouraged! Your faith has made you well." And the woman was healed at that moment.

Matthew 9:22 NLT

Genuine faith is never meant to be locked up in the heart of a believer; to the contrary, it is meant to be shared with the world. But, if you sincerely seek to share your faith, you must first find it.

When a suffering woman sought healing by merely touching the hem of His cloak, Jesus replied, "Daughter, be of good comfort; thy faith hath made thee whole" (Matthew 9:22 KJV). The message to believers of every generation is clear: live by faith today and every day.

How can you strengthen your faith? Through praise, through worship, through Bible study, and through prayer. And, as your faith becomes stronger, you will find ways to share it with your friends, your family, and with the world. When you place your faith, your trust, indeed your life in the hands of Christ Jesus, you'll be amazed at the marvelous things He can do with you and through you; so trust God's plans. With Him, all things are possible, and whatever "it" is, God is bigger.

TODAY IS YOUR CLASSROOM

If you teach the wise, they will get knowledge.

Proverbs 21:11 NCV

Today is your classroom: what will you learn? Will you use today's experiences as tools for personal growth, or will you ignore the lessons that life and God are trying to teach you? Will you seek to follow God's will today, with your eyes and your heart open? Will you carefully study God's Word, and will you apply His teachings to the experiences of everyday life? Hopefully so. After all, the events of today have much to teach. And you still have much to learn.

May you live—and learn—accordingly.

—.—.—.—.—.—.—.—

True learning can take place at every age of life, and it doesn't have to be in the curriculum plan.

Suzanne Dale Ezell

MIDCOURSE CORRECTIONS

The wise see danger ahead and avoid it, but fools keep going and get into trouble.

Proverbs 22:3 NCV

In our fast-paced world, everyday life has become an exercise in managing change. Our circumstances change; our relationships change; our bodies change. We grow older every day, as does our world. Thankfully, God does not change. He is eternal, as are the truths that are found in His Holy Word.

Are you facing one of life's inevitable "mid-course corrections"? If so, you must place your faith, your trust, and your life in the hands of the One who does not change: your Heavenly Father. He is the unmoving rock upon which you must construct this day and every day. When you do, you are secure.

—·—·—·—·—·—·—

The God who orchestrates the universe has a good many things to consider that have not occurred to me, and it is well that I leave them to Him.

Elisabeth Elliot

GOD'S SURPRISING PLANS

But as it is written: What no eye has seen and no ear has heard, and what has never come into a man's heart, is what God has prepared for those who love Him.

1 Corinthians 2:9 Holman CSB

God has plans for your life, wonderful, surprising plans . . . but He won't force those plans upon you. To the contrary, He has given you free will, the ability to make decisions on your own. With that freedom to choose comes the responsibility of living with the consequences of the choices you make.

If you seek to live in accordance with God's will for your life—and you should—then you will live in accordance with His commandments. You will study God's Word, and you will be watchful for His signs. You will associate with fellow Christians who will encourage your spiritual growth, and you will listen to that inner voice that speaks to you in the quiet moments of your daily devotionals.

God intends to use you in wonderful, unexpected ways if you let Him. The decision to seek God's plan and to follow it is yours and yours alone. The consequences of that decision have implications that are both profound and eternal, so choose carefully.

TODAY: A DAY OF CELEBRATION

This is the day the Lord has made; let us rejoice and be glad in it.

Psalm 118:24 Holman CSB

God gives us this day; He fills it to the brim with possibilities, and He challenges us to use it for His purposes. The 118th Psalm reminds us that today, like every other day, is a cause for celebration. The day is presented to us fresh and clean at midnight, free of charge, but we must beware: Today is a non-renewable resource—once it's gone, it's gone forever. Our responsibility, of course, is to use this day in the service of God's will and according to His commandments.

Today, treasure the time that God has given you. Give Him the glory and the praise and the thanksgiving that He deserves. And search for the hidden possibilities that God has placed along your path. This day is a priceless gift from God, so use it joyfully and encourage others to do likewise. After all, this is the day the Lord has made.

—.—.—.—.—.—.—

If you can forgive the person you were, accept the person you are, and believe in the person you will become, you are headed for joy. So celebrate your life.

Barbara Johnson

GOD'S WISDOM: AN ENDLESS FOUNTAIN

Understanding is like a fountain which gives life to those who use it.

Proverbs 16:22 NCV

Where will you place your trust today? Will you seek guidance from fallible friends and acquaintances— friends who may be well meaning but who are highly imperfect? Or will you do the smart thing by placing your faith in God's perfect wisdom? When you decide whom to trust, you will then know how best to respond to the challenges of the coming day.

Are you tired? Discouraged? Fearful? Be comforted and trust God. Are you worried or anxious? Be confident in God's power and trust His Holy Word. Are you confused? Listen to the quiet voice of your Heavenly Father. He is not a God of confusion. Talk with Him; listen to Him; trust Him. He is steadfast, and He is your Protector . . . forever.

—.—.—.—.—.—.—

No matter how many books you read, no matter how many schools you attend, you're never really wise until you start making wise choices.

Marie T. Freeman

LIVING WITH THE UNEXPECTED

Do not boast about tomorrow, for you do not know what a day may bring forth.

Proverbs 27:1 NKJV

The old saying is both familiar and true: "Man proposes and God disposes." Proverbs 27:1 reminds us that our world unfolds according to God's plans, not our wishes. Thus, boasting about future events is to be avoided by those who acknowledge God's sovereignty over all things.

Are you planning for a better tomorrow for yourself and your family? If so, you are to be congratulated: God rewards forethought in the same way that He often punishes impulsiveness. But as you make your plans, do so with humility, with gratitude, and with trust in your Heavenly Father. His hand directs the future; to think otherwise is both arrogant and naïve.

—.—.—.—.—.—.—

Like little children on Christmas Eve, we know that lovely surprises are in the making. We can't see them. We have simply been told, and we believe. Tomorrow we shall see.

Elisabeth Elliot

YOUR PLANS, GOD'S PLANS

You reveal the path of life to me; in Your presence is abundant joy; in Your right hand are eternal pleasures.

Psalm 16:11 Holman CSB

God has things He wants you to do and places He wants you to go. The most important decision of your life is, of course, your commitment to accept Jesus Christ as your personal Lord and Savior. And, once your eternal destiny is secured, you will undoubtedly ask yourself the question "What now, Lord?" If you earnestly seek God's will for your life, you will find it . . . in time.

As you seek to discover God's path for your life, you should study His Holy Word and be ever watchful for His signs. You should associate with fellow Christians who will encourage your spiritual growth, and you should listen to that inner voice that speaks to you in the quiet moments of your daily devotionals.

Rest assured: God is here, and He intends to use you in wonderful, unexpected ways. He desires to lead you along a path of His choosing. Your challenge is to watch, to listen . . . and to follow.

—.—.—.—.—.—.—.—

Yesterday is just experience, but tomorrow is glistening with purpose—and today is the channel leading from one to the other.

Barbara Johnson

A FAITH BIGGER THAN FEAR

Do not let your hearts be troubled. Trust in God; trust also in me. In my Father's house are many rooms; if it were not so, I would have told you. I am going there to prepare a place for you.

John 14:1-2 NIV

Because we are imperfect human beings, we worry. Even though we are Christians who have been given the assurance of salvation—even though we are Christians who have received the promise of God's love and protection—we find ourselves fretting over the countless details of everyday life. Jesus understood our concerns when He spoke the reassuring words found in Matthew 6: "Therefore I tell you, do not worry about your life . . ."

As you consider the promises of Jesus, remember that God still sits in His heaven and you are His beloved child. Then, perhaps, you will worry a little less and trust God a little more, and that's as it should be because God is trustworthy . . . and you are protected.

—.—.—.—.—.—.—

Submit each day to God, knowing that He is God over all your tomorrows.

Kay Arthur

FINDING FULFILLMENT IN ALL THE RIGHT PLACES

I am the door. If anyone enters by Me, he will be saved, and will come in and go out and find pasture.

John 10:9-11 Holman CSB

Where can we find contentment? Is it a result of wealth or power or beauty or fame? Hardly. Genuine contentment is a gift from God to those who trust Him and follow His commandments.

Our modern world seems preoccupied with the search for happiness. We are bombarded with messages telling us that happiness depends upon the acquisition of material possessions. These messages are false. Enduring peace is not the result of our acquisitions; it is a spiritual gift from God to those who obey Him and accept His will.

If we don't find contentment in God, we will never find it anywhere else. But, if we seek Him and obey Him, we will be blessed with an inner peace that is beyond human understanding. When God dwells at the center of our lives, peace and contentment will belong to us just as surely as we belong to God.

SELF-ESTEEM 101

Therefore, we may boldly say: The Lord is my helper; I will not be afraid. What can man do to me?

Hebrews 13:6 Holman CSB

Sometimes, it's hard to feel good about yourself, especially since you live in a society that keeps sending out the message that you've got to be perfect.

Are you your own worst critic? And in response to that criticism, are you constantly trying to transform yourself into a young woman who meets society's expectations, but not God's expectations? If so, it's time to become a little more understanding of the person in the mirror.

Millions of words have been written about various ways to improve self-esteem. Yet, maintaining a healthy self-image is, to a surprising extent, a matter of doing a few simple things: 1. Obeying God. 2. Thinking healthy thoughts. 3. Finding things to do that please your Creator and yourself. 4. Finding encouraging friends who reinforce your sense of self-worth, friends who urge you to behave yourself and believe in yourself. When you do these things, your self-image will to take care of itself.

—·—·—·—·—·—·—

Being loved by Him whose opinion matters most gives us the security to risk loving, too—even loving ourselves.

Gloria Gaither

THE COURAGE TO FOLLOW GOD

Be strong and courageous, and do the work. Don't be afraid or discouraged, for the Lord God, my God, is with you. He won't leave you or forsake you.

1 Chronicles 28:20 Holman CSB

Christians have every reason to live courageously. After all, the ultimate battle has already been won on the cross at Calvary. But even dedicated followers of Christ may find their courage tested by the inevitable disappointments and fears that visit the lives of believers and non-believers alike.

When you find yourself worried about the challenges of today or the uncertainties of tomorrow, you must ask yourself whether or not you are ready to place your concerns and your life in God's all-powerful, all-knowing, all-loving hands. If the answer to that question is yes—as it should be—then you can draw courage today from the source of strength that never fails: your Heavenly Father.

—.—.—.—.—.—.—

Just as courage is faith in good, so discouragement is faith in evil, and, while courage opens the door to good, discouragement opens it to evil.

Hannah Whitall Smith

WELCOMING THE NEW YOU

You were taught to leave your old self—to stop living the evil way you lived before. That old self becomes worse, because people are fooled by the evil things they want to do. But you were taught to be made new in your hearts, to become a new person. That new person is made to be like God—made to be truly good and holy.

Ephesians 4:22–24 NCV

Think, for a moment, about the "old" you, the person you were before you invited Christ to reign over your heart. Now, think about the "new" you, the person you have become since then. Is there a difference between the "old" you and the "new and improved" version? There should be! And that difference should be noticeable not only to you but also to others.

The Bible clearly teaches that when we welcome Christ into our hearts, we become new creations through Him. Our challenge, of course, is to behave ourselves like new creations. When we do, God fills our hearts, He blesses our endeavors, and transforms our lives . . . forever.

—.—.—.—.—.—.—

Shake the dust from your past, and move forward in His promises.

Kay Arthur

A HEALTHY FEAR

Reverence for the Lord is the foundation of true wisdom.
The rewards of wisdom come to all who obey him.

Psalm 111:10 NLT

The Bible instructs us that a healthy fear of the Lord is the foundation of wisdom. Yet sometimes, in our shortsightedness, we fail to show respect for our Creator because we fail to obey Him. When we do, our disobedience always has consequences, and sometimes those consequences are severe.

When we honor the Father by obeying His commandments, we receive His love and His grace. Today, let us demonstrate our respect for God by developing a healthy fear of disobeying Him.

—.—.—.—.—.—.—

When once we are assured that God is good, then there can be nothing left to fear.

Hannah Whitall Smith

THE ULTIMATE ARMOR

Finally, be strong in the Lord and in his mighty power. Put on the full armor of God so that you can take your stand against the devil's schemes.

Ephesians 6:10-11 NIV

In a world filled with dangers and temptations, God is the ultimate armor. In a world filled with misleading messages, God's Word is the ultimate truth. In a world filled with more frustrations than we can count, God's Son offers the ultimate peace. Will you accept God's peace and wear God's armor against the dangers of our world?

Sometimes, in the crush of everyday life, God may seem far away, but He is not. God is everywhere you have ever been and everywhere you will ever go. He is with you night and day; He knows your thoughts and your prayers. He is your ultimate Protector. And, when you earnestly seek His protection, you will find it because He is here—always—waiting patiently for you to reach out to Him.

—·—·—·—·—·—·—

He goes before us, follows behind us, and hems us safe inside the realm of His protection.

Beth Moore

USING OUR GIFTS

I remind you to keep using the gift God gave you . . . .
Now let it grow, as a small flame grows into a fire.

2 Timothy 1:6 NCV

Your talents, resources, and opportunities are all gifts from the Giver of all things good. And the best way to say "Thank You" for these gifts is to use them.

Do you have a particular talent? Hone your skill and use it. Do you possess financial resources? Share them. Have you been blessed by a particular opportunity, or have you experienced unusual good fortune? Use your good fortune to help others.

When you share the gifts God has given you—and when you share them freely and without fanfare—you invite God to bless you more and more. So today, do yourself and the world a favor: be a faithful steward of your talents and treasures. And then prepare yourself for even greater blessings that are sure to come.

—.—.—.—.—.—.—

The Lord has abundantly blessed me all of my life. I'm not trying to pay Him back for all of His wonderful gifts; I just realize that He gave them to me to give away.

Lisa Whelchel

THOUGHTFUL WORDS

The wise store up knowledge, but the mouth of the fool hastens destruction.

Proverbs 10:14 Holman CSB

Think . . . pause . . . then speak: How wise is the person who can communicate in this way. But all too often, in the rush to have ourselves heard, we speak first and think next . . . with unfortunate results.

God's Word reminds us that, "Reckless words pierce like a sword, but the tongue of the wise brings healing" (Proverbs 12:18 NIV). If we seek to be a source of encouragement to friends and family, then we must measure our words carefully. Words are important: they can hurt or heal. Words can uplift us or discourage us, and reckless words, spoken in haste, cannot be erased.

Today, seek to encourage all who cross your path. Measure your words carefully. Speak wisely, not impulsively. Use words of kindness and praise, not words of anger or derision. Remember that you have the power to heal others or to injure them, to lift others up or to hold them back. When you lift them up, your wisdom will bring healing and comfort to a world that needs both.

—·—·—·—·—·—·—

A little kindly advice is better than a great deal of scolding.

Fanny Crosby

POPULARITY CONTESTS

*Do you think I am trying to make people accept me?
No, God is the One I am trying to please. Am I trying to
please people? If I still wanted to please people, I would
not be a servant of Christ.*

Galatians 1:10 NCV

Are you a people-pleaser or a God-pleaser? Hopefully, you're far more concerned with pleasing God than you are with pleasing your friends. But face facts: even if you're a devoted Christian, you're still going to feel the urge to impress your friends and acquaintances—and sometimes that urge will be strong.

Peer pressure can be good or bad, depending upon who your peers are and how they behave. If your friends encourage you to follow God's will and to obey His commandments, then you'll experience positive peer pressure, and that's a good thing. But, if your friends encourage you to do foolish things, then you're facing a different kind of peer pressure . . . and you'd better beware.

To sum it up, here's your choice: you can choose to please God first, or you can fall victim to peer pressure. The choice is yours—and so are the consequences.

—.—.—.—.—.—

Those who follow the crowd usually get lost in it.

Rick Warren

SELF-DEFEATING ANGER

When you are angry, do not sin, and be sure to stop being angry before the end of the day. Do not give the devil a way to defeat you.

Ephesians 4:26–27 NCV

Perhaps God gave each of us one mouth and two ears in order that we might listen twice as much as we speak. Unfortunately, many of us do otherwise, especially when we become angry.

Anger is a natural human emotion that is sometimes necessary and appropriate. Even Jesus Himself became angered when He confronted the moneychangers in the temple. But, more often than not, our frustrations are of the more mundane variety.

As long as we live, we will inevitably face countless opportunities to lose our tempers over small, relatively insignificant events: an inconsiderate driver, a spilled cup of milk, an unfortunate comment, a forgotten promise. These sorts of frustrations may irritate us, but they should not conquer us. We should conquer them.

—·—·—·—·—·—

When something robs you of your peace of mind, ask yourself if it is worth the energy you are expending on it. If not, then put it out of your mind in an act of discipline. Every time the thought of "it" returns, refuse it.

Kay Arthur

SLOW DOWN

The plans of the diligent certainly lead to profit, but anyone who is reckless only becomes poor.

Proverbs 21:5 Holman CSB

Everybody knows you're a very busy young woman. But here's a question: are you able to squeeze time into your hectic schedule for God? Hopefully so! But if you're one of those who rush through the day with scarcely a single moment to talk with your Creator, it's time to reshuffle your priorities.

You live in a noisy world, a world filled with distractions, frustrations, temptations, and complications. But if you allow the distractions of everyday life to distract you from God's peace, you're doing yourself a big disservice. So here's some good advice: instead of rushing nonstop through the day, slow yourself down long enough to have a few quiet minutes with God.

Nothing is more important than the time you spend with your Heavenly Father. Absolutely nothing. So be still and claim the inner peace that is your spiritual birthright: the peace of Jesus Christ. It is offered freely; it has been paid for in full; it is yours for the asking. So ask. And then share.

THE DANGERS OF PRIDE

Pride leads only to shame; it is wise to be humble.

Proverbs 11:2 NCV

The words from Proverbs 11 remind us that pride and destruction are traveling partners. But as imperfect human beings, we are tempted to puff out our chests and crow about our own accomplishments. When we do so, we delude ourselves.

As Christians, we have a profound reason to be humble: We have been refashioned and saved by Jesus Christ, and that salvation came not because of our own good works but because of God's grace. Thus, we are not "self-made," we are "God-made" and "Christ-saved." How, then, can we be boastful? The answer, of course, is simple: if we are honest with ourselves and with our God, we cannot be boastful. In the quiet moments, when we search the depths of our own hearts, we know that whatever "it" is, God did that. And He deserves the credit.

—.—.—.—.—.—.—

All kindness and good deeds, we must keep silent. The result will be an inner reservoir of personality power.

Catherine Marshall

FORGIVENESS AND SPIRITUAL GROWTH

Be gentle with one another, sensitive. Forgive one another as quickly and thoroughly as God in Christ forgave you.

Ephesians 4:32 MSG

Are you the kind of girl who has a tough time forgiving and forgetting? If so, welcome to the club. Most of us find it difficult to forgive the people who have hurt us. And that's too bad because life would be much simpler if we could forgive people "once and for all" and be done with it. Yet forgiveness is seldom that easy. Usually, the decision to forgive is straightforward, but the process of forgiving is more difficult. Forgiveness is a journey that requires effort, time, perseverance, and prayer.

If there exists even one person whom you have not forgiven (and that includes yourself), obey God's commandment: forgive that person today. And remember that bitterness, anger, and regret are not part of God's plan for your life. Forgiveness is.

If you sincerely wish to forgive someone, pray for that person. And then pray for yourself by asking God to heal your heart. Don't expect forgiveness to be easy or quick, but rest assured: with God as your partner, you can forgive . . . and you will.

PERSEVERING FOR GOD

Thanks be to God! He gives us the victory through our Lord Jesus Christ. Therefore, my dear brothers, stand firm. Let nothing move you. Always give yourselves fully to the work of the Lord, because you know that your labor in the Lord is not in vain.

1 Corinthians 15:57-58 NIV

Are you a girl who doesn't give up easily, or are you quick to bail out when the going gets tough? If you've developed the unfortunate habit of giving up at the first sign of trouble, it's probably time for you to have a heart-to-heart talk with that person you see every time you look in the mirror.

A well-lived life is like a marathon, not a sprint—it calls for preparation, determination, and lots of perseverance. As an example of perfect perseverance, you need look no further than your Savior, Jesus Christ.

Jesus finished what He began. Despite His suffering and despite the shame of the cross, Jesus was steadfast in His faithfulness to God. You, too, should remain faithful, especially when times are tough.

Are you facing a difficult situation? If so, remember this: whatever your problem, God can handle it. Your job is to keep persevering until He does.

CHOICES MATTER

But Daniel purposed in his heart that he would not defile himself . . . .

Daniel 1:8 KJV

Every life, including yours, is a tapestry of choices. And the quality of your life depends, to a surprising extent, on the quality of the choices you make.

Would you like to enjoy a life of abundance and significance? If so, you must make choices that are pleasing to God.

From the instant you wake up in the morning until the moment you nod off to sleep at night, you make lots of decisions: decisions about the things you do, decisions about the words you speak, and decisions about the thoughts you choose to think.

Today and every day, it's up to you (and only you) to make wise choices, choices that enhance your relationship with God. After all, He deserves no less than your best . . . and neither do you.

—.—.—.—.—.—.—

There may be no trumpet sound or loud applause when we make a right decision, just a calm sense of resolution and peace.

Gloria Gaither

ENERGY FOR TODAY

Let us lay aside every weight and the sin that so easily ensnares us, and run with endurance the race that lies before us, keeping our eyes on Jesus, the source and perfecter of our faith.

Hebrews 12:1-2 Holman CSB

All of us have moments when we feel drained. All of us suffer through difficult days, trying times, and perplexing periods of our lives. Thankfully, God stands ready and willing to give us comfort and strength if we turn to Him.

Burning the candle at both ends is tempting but potentially destructive. Instead, we should place first things first by saying no to the things that we simply don't have the time or the energy to do. As we establish our priorities, we should turn to God and to His Holy Word for guidance.

If you're a person with too many demands and too few hours in which to meet them, don't fret. Instead, focus upon God and upon His love for you. Then, ask Him for the wisdom to prioritize your life and the strength to fulfill your responsibilities. God will give you the energy to do the most important things on today's to-do list . . . if you ask Him. So ask Him.

CHOOSING (AND DATING) WISELY

The thing you should want most is God's kingdom and doing what God wants. Then all these other things you need will be given to you.

Matthew 6:33 NCV

The choices you make will determine the quality and direction of your life. And that includes all the choices you make about your dating life. As an informed citizen of the 21st century, you have every reason to make wise choices. But sometimes, when the pressures of the dating world threaten to grind you up and spit you out, you may feel tempted to make decisions that are displeasing to God. When you do, you'll suffer in more ways than you can imagine.

So, as you pause to consider the kind of Christian you are—and the kind of Christian you want to become—ask yourself whether you're sitting on the fence or standing in the light. And then, if you sincerely want to follow in the footsteps of the One from Galilee, make choices that are pleasing to Him. He deserves no less . . . and neither, for that matter, do you.

—·—·—·—·—·—·—

Freedom is not the right to do what we want but the power to do what we ought.

Corrie ten Boom

WHEN YOU ARE HURT

We take the good days from God—why not also the bad days?

Job 2:10 MSG

Face it: sometimes people can be cruel . . . very cruel. When other people are unkind to you or to your friends, you may be tempted to strike back, either verbally or in some other way. Don't do it! Instead, remember that God corrects other people's behaviors in His own way, and He doesn't need your help (even if you're totally convinced that He does!). Remember that God has commanded you to forgive others, just as you, too, must sometimes seek forgiveness from others.

So, when other people behave cruelly, foolishly, or impulsively—as they will from time to time—don't be a hotheaded girl. Instead, speak up for yourself as politely as you can, and walk away. Then, forgive everybody as quickly as you can, and leave the rest up to God.

—.—.—.—.—.—.—

Some folks cause happiness wherever they go, others whenever they go.

Barbara Johnson

DOING THE RIGHT THING

And you shall do what is good and right in the sight of the Lord, that it may be well with you . . . .

Deuteronomy 6:18 NASB

Everyday life is an adventure in decision-making. Each day, we make countless decisions that hopefully bring us closer to God. When we live according to God's commandments, we share in His abundance and His peace. But, when we turn our backs upon God by disobeying Him, we bring needless suffering upon ourselves and upon our families.

Do you seek God's peace and His blessings? Then obey Him. When you're faced with a difficult choice or a powerful temptation, seek God's counsel and trust the counsel He gives. Invite God into your heart and live according to His commandments. When you do, you will be blessed today, and tomorrow, and forever.

—·—·—·—·—·—·—

He doesn't need an abundance of words. He doesn't need a dissertation about your life. He just wants your attention. He wants your heart.

Kathy Troccoli

A HEART PREPARED FOR PRAYER

But when you are praying, first forgive anyone you are holding a grudge against, so that your Father in heaven will forgive your sins, too.

Mark 11:25 NLT

Life is a patchwork of successes and failures, victories and defeats, joys and sorrows. When we experience life's inevitable disappointments, we may become embittered, but God instructs us to do otherwise. God understands the futility of bitterness, and He knows that without forgiveness, we can never enjoy the spiritual abundance that He offers us through the person of His Son Jesus.

Christ's teachings are straightforward: Before we offer our prayers to God, we should cleanse ourselves of bitterness, hatred, jealousy, and regret. When we do so, we can petition God with pure hearts.

—.—.—.—.—.—.—

Sin is any deed or memory that hampers or binds human personality.

Catherine Marshall

THE GIFT OF GRACE

*For it is by grace you have been saved, through faith—
and this not from yourselves, it is the gift of God . . . .*

Ephesians 2:8 NIV

God has given us so many gifts, but none can compare with the gift of salvation. We have not earned our salvation; it is a gift from God. When we accept Christ into our hearts, we are saved by His grace.

The familiar words of Ephesians 2:8 make God's promise perfectly clear: It is by grace we have been saved, through faith. We are saved not because of our good deeds but because of our faith in Christ.

God's grace is the ultimate gift, and we owe to Him the ultimate in thanksgiving. Let us praise the Creator for His priceless gift, and let us share the Good News with all who cross our paths. We return our Father's love by accepting His grace and by sharing His message and His love. When we do, we are eternally blessed . . . and the Father smiles.

—.—.—.—.—.—.—.—

God does amazing works through prayers that seek to extend His grace to others.

Shirley Dobson

MATERIAL AND SPIRITUAL POSSESSIONS

And how do you benefit if you gain the whole world but lose your own soul in the process? Is anything worth more than your soul?

Mark 8:36-37 NLT

It seems like the whole world is focused on money and the stuff money can buy. But earthly riches are temporary: here today and soon gone forever. Spiritual riches, on the other hand, are permanent: ours today, ours tomorrow, ours throughout eternity.

Our material possessions have the potential to do great good or terrible harm, depending upon how we choose to use them. As believers, our instructions are clear: we must use our possessions in accordance with God's commandments, and we must be faithful stewards of the gifts He has seen fit to bestow upon us.

Today, let us honor God by placing no other gods before Him. God comes first; everything else comes next—and "everything else" most certainly includes all of our earthly possessions.

—·—·—·—·—·—·—

I have held many things in my hands, and I have lost them all; but whatever I have placed in God's hands, that I still possess.

Corrie ten Boom

WHERE THE SPIRIT LEADS

The true children of God are those who let God's Spirit lead them.

Romans 8:14 NCV

Paul encourages believers to be filled with the Spirit of God: "Do not be drunk with wine, which will ruin you, but be filled with the Spirit" (Ephesians 5:18). When you are filled with the Holy Spirit, your words and deeds will reflect a love and devotion to Christ. When you are filled with the Holy Spirit, the steps of your life's journey are guided by the Lord. When you allow God's Spirit to work in you and through you, you will be energized and transformed.

Today, allow yourself to be filled with the Spirit of God. And then stand back in amazement as God begins to work miracles in your own life and in the lives of those you love.

—.—.—.—.—.—.—.—

Are you experiencing prayer problems? The Holy Spirit will help you. When we are totally inadequate, the Spirit is interceding with God the Father for us.

Corrie ten Boom

GOOD TREASURE FROM A GOOD HEART

A good person produces good deeds and words season after season.

Matthew 12:35 MSG

How can we demonstrate our love for God? By accepting His Son as our personal Savior and by placing Christ squarely at the center of our lives and our hearts. Jesus said that if we are to love Him, we must obey His commandments (John 14:15). Thus, our obedience to the Master is an expression of our love for Him.

In Ephesians 2:10 we read, "For we are His workmanship, created in Christ Jesus for good works" (NKJV). These words are instructive: We are not saved by good works, but for good works. Good works are not the root, but rather the fruit of our salvation.

Today, let the fruits of your stewardship be a clear demonstration of your love for Christ. When you do, your good heart will bring forth many good things for yourself and for God. Christ has given you spiritual abundance and eternal life. You, in turn, owe Him good treasure from a single obedient heart . . . yours.

—·—·—·—·—·—·—

Light is stronger than darkness—darkness cannot "comprehend" or "overcome" it.

Anne Graham Lotz

JESUS IS FIRST

First pay attention to me, and then relax. Now you can take it easy—you're in good hands.

Proverbs 1:33 MSG

Here's a tip for your dating life: behave yourself like a Christian every day of the week, not just on Sundays. In other words, make Jesus a priority in every aspect of your life, including your dating life.

Jesus made an extreme sacrifice for you. Are you willing to make changes in your life for Him? Can you honestly say that you're passionate about your faith and that you're really following Jesus? Hopefully so. But if you're preoccupied with other things—or if you're strictly a one-day-a-week Christian—then you're in need of a big time spiritual makeover.

Jesus doesn't want you to be a run-of-the-mill, follow-the-crowd kind of believer. Jesus wants you to be a "new creation" through Him. And that's exactly what you should want for yourself, too.

So remember this: you're the recipient of Christ's love. Accept it enthusiastically and demonstrate your love with words and actions. Jesus deserves your heart—give it to Him today, tomorrow, and forever, Amen.

FINDING (AND TRUSTING) MENTORS

A wise man will hear and increase in learning, and a man of understanding will acquire wise counsel.

Proverbs 1:5 NASB

Do you want to become wise? Then you must acknowledge that you are not wise enough on your own. When you face an important decision, you must first study God's Word, and you should also seek the counsel of trusted friends and mentors.

When we arrive at the inevitable crossroads of life, God inevitably sends righteous men and women to guide us if we let them. If we are willing to listen and to learn, then we, too, will become wise. And God will bless our endeavors.

—.—.—.—.—.—.—.—

He teaches us, not just to let us see ourselves correctly, but to help us see him correctly.

Kathy Troccoli

DEMONSTRATING YOUR FAITH

So brothers and sisters, be careful that none of you has an evil, unbelieving heart that will turn you away from the living God. But encourage each other every day while it is "today." Help each other so none of you will become hardened because sin has tricked you.

Hebrews 3:13 NCV

Let's face facts: those of us who are Christians should be willing to talk about the things that Christ has done for us. Our personal testimonies are vitally important, but sometimes, because of shyness or insecurities, we're afraid to share our experiences. And that's unfortunate.

In his second letter to Timothy, Paul shares a message to believers of every generation when he writes, "God has not given us a spirit of timidity" (1:7). Paul's meaning is crystal clear: When sharing our testimonies, we must be courageous and unashamed.

We live in a world that desperately needs the healing message of Christ Jesus. Every believer, each in his or her own way, bears responsibility for sharing the Good News of our Savior. And it is important to remember that we bear testimony through both words and actions.

If you seek to be a radical follower of Christ, then it's time for you to share your testimony with others. So today, preach the Gospel through your words and your deeds . . . but not necessarily in that order.

THE DAILY PATH

Then He said to them all, "If anyone wants to come with Me, he must deny himself, take up his cross daily, and follow Me."

Luke 9:23 Holman CSB

There's an old saying—trite but true—"Today is the first day of the rest of your life." Whatever your situation may be, remember that this day holds boundless possibilities if you are wise enough and observant enough to claim them.

For believers, every day begins and ends with God and His Son. Christ came to this earth to give us abundant life and eternal salvation. Our task is to accept Christ's grace with joy in our hearts and praise on our lips. Believers who fashion their days around Jesus are transformed: They see the world differently, they act differently, and they feel differently about themselves and their neighbors.

Christians face the inevitable challenges and disappointments of each day armed with the joy of Christ and the promise of salvation. So whatever this day holds for you, begin it and end it with God as your partner and Christ as your Savior. And throughout the day, give thanks to the One who created you and saved you. God's love for you is infinite. Accept it joyously and be thankful.

EXPECTING THE IMPOSSIBLE

Is anything impossible for the Lord?

Genesis 18:14 Holman CSB

Do you believe that God is at work in the world? And do you believe that nothing is impossible for Him? If so, then you also believe that God is perfectly capable of doing things that you, as a mere human being with limited vision and limited understanding, would deem to be utterly impossible. And that's precisely what God does.

Since He created our universe out of nothingness, God has made a habit of doing miraculous things. And He still works miracles today. Expect Him to work miracles in your own life, and then be watchful. With God, absolutely nothing is impossible, including an amazing assortment of miracles that He stands ready, willing, and able to perform for you.

—.—.—.—.—.—.—

If all things are possible with God, then all things are possible to him who believes in him.

Corrie ten Boom

THE JOYS OF A CLEAR CONSCIENCE

Let us come near to God with a sincere heart and a sure faith, because we have been made free from a guilty conscience, and our bodies have been washed with pure water.

Hebrews 10:22 NCV

Billy Graham correctly observed, "Most of us follow our conscience as we follow a wheelbarrow. We push it in front of us in the direction we want to go." To do so, of course, is a profound mistake. Yet all of us, on occasion, have failed to listen to the voice that God planted in our hearts, and all of us have suffered the consequences.

God gave you a conscience for a very good reason: to make your path conform to His will. Wise believers make it a practice to listen carefully to that quiet internal voice. Count yourself among that number. When your conscience speaks, listen and learn. In all likelihood, God is trying to get His message through. And in all likelihood, it is a message that you desperately need to hear.

—·—·—·—·—·—

Your conscience is your alarm system. It's your protection.

Charles Stanley

ARE YOU DATING? BE PICKY!

Do not be unequally yoked together with unbelievers.
For what fellowship has righteousness with lawlessness?
And what communion has light with darkness?

2 Corinthians 6:14 NKJV

If you're still searching for Mr. Right (while trying to avoid falling in love with Mr. Wrong), be patient, be prudent, and be picky. Look for a guy whose values you respect, whose behavior you approve of, and whose faith you admire. Remember that appearances can be deceiving and tempting, so watch your step. And when it comes to the important task of building a lifetime relationship with the guy of your dreams, pray about it!

If you happen to be one of those very lucky girls who has already fallen madly in love with the same wonderful guy who has (coincidentally) already fallen madly in love with you, say a great big thanks to the Matchmaker in heaven. But if you haven't yet found Mr. Right, don't fret. Just keep trusting God, and keep yourself open to the direction in which He is leading you. And remember: When it comes to selecting a man, God wants to give His approval—or not—but He won't give it until He's asked. So ask, listen, and decide accordingly.

WHEN WE ARE BLESSED, WE ARE TESTED

Blessed in the man who does not walk in the counsel of the wicked or stand in the way of sinners or sit in the seat of mockers. But his delight is in the law of the Lord, and on his law he meditates day and night. He is like a tree planted by streams of water, which yields its fruit in season and whose leaf does not wither. Whatever he does prospers.

Psalm 1:1-3 NIV

Sometimes, we are tested more by prosperity than by poverty. When we experience life's difficult days, we may be more likely to turn our thoughts and hearts to God. But in times of plenty, when the sun is shining and our minds are at ease, we may be tempted to believe that our good fortune is entirely of our own making. Nothing could be further from the truth. God plays a hand in every aspect of everyday life, and for the blessings that we receive, we must offer thanks and praise to Him, not to ourselves.

Have you been blessed by God? Are you enjoying the abundance He has promised? If so, praise Him for His gifts. Praise Him faithfully and humbly. And don't, for a single moment, allow a prideful heart to separate you from the blessings of your loving Father.

DABBLERS BEWARE

I do not consider myself yet to have taken hold of it. But one thing I do: Forgetting what is behind and straining toward what is ahead, I press on toward the goal to win the prize for which God has called me heavenward in Christ Jesus.

Philippians 3:13-14 NIV

Is Christ the focus of your life? Are you fired with enthusiasm for Him? Are you an energized Christian who allows God's Son to reign over every aspect of your day? Make no mistake: that's exactly what God intends for you to do.

God has given you the gift of eternal life through His Son. In response to God's priceless gift, you are instructed to focus your thoughts, your prayers, and your energies upon God and His only begotten Son. To do so, you must resist the subtle yet powerful temptation to become a "spiritual dabbler."

A person who dabbles in the Christian faith is unwilling to place God in His rightful place: above all other things. Resist that temptation; make God the cornerstone and the touchstone of your life. When you do, He will give you all the strength and wisdom you need to live victoriously for Him.

HOW OFTEN DO YOU ASK?

Ask and it will be given to you; seek and you will find; knock and the door will be opened to you. For everyone who asks receives; he who seeks finds; and to him who knocks, the door will be opened.

Matthew 7:7-8 NIV

How often do you ask for God's help? Occasionally? Intermittently? Whenever you experience a crisis? Hopefully not. Hopefully, you have developed the habit of asking for God's assistance early and often. And hopefully, you have learned to seek His guidance in every aspect of your life.

God has promised that when you ask for His help, He will not withhold it. So ask. Ask Him to meet the needs of your day. Ask Him for wisdom. Ask Him to lead you, to protect you, and to correct you. And trust the answers He gives.

God stands at the door and waits. When you knock on His door, He answers. Your task, of course, is to seek His guidance prayerfully, confidently, and often.

—.—.—.—.—.—.—

We get into trouble when we think we know what to do and we stop asking God if we're doing it.

Stormie Omartian

FOR GOD SO LOVED THE WORLD

This is how much God loved the world: He gave his Son, his one and only Son. And this is why: so that no one need be destroyed; by believing in him anyone can have a whole and lasting life.

John 3:16 MSG

For Christians, death is not an ending; it is a beginning. For Christian believers, the grave is not a final resting-place; it is a place of transition. Yet even when we know our loved ones are at peace with Christ, we still weep bitter tears, not so much for the departed, but instead for ourselves.

God promises that He is "close to the brokenhearted" (Psalm 34:18). In times of intense sadness, we must turn to Him, and we must encourage our friends and family members to do likewise. Death can never claim those who have accepted Christ as their personal Savior. We have received the gift of life abundant and eternal.

—·—·—·—·—·—·—

Considering how I prepare for my children when I know they are coming home, I love to think of the preparations God is making for my homecoming one day. He knows the colors I love, the scenery I enjoy, the things that make me happy, all the personal details.

Anne Graham Lotz

WHO SHOULD YOU PLEASE?

A tranquil heart is life to the body, but jealousy is rottenness to the bones.

Proverbs 14:30 Holman CSB

Sometimes, it's very tempting to be a people-pleaser. But usually, it's the wrong thing to do.

When you worry too much about pleasing dates or friends, you may not worry enough about pleasing God—and when you fail to please God, you inevitably pay a very high price for your mistaken priorities.

Whom will you try to please today: God or your friends? Your obligation is most certainly not to your peers or to your date. Your obligation is to an all-knowing and perfect God. Trust Him always. Love Him always. Praise Him always. And seek to please Him and only Him. Always.

—·—·—·—·—·—

It is comfortable to know that we are responsible to God and not to man. It is a small matter to be judged of man's judgement.

Lottie Moon

DO THE RIGHT THING

You can't pick and choose in these things, specializing in keeping one or two things in God's law and ignoring others.

James 2:10 MSG

If you continue to date somebody who behaves foolishly or impulsively, then sooner or later, you'll probably find yourself doing impulsive things, too. And that's bad . . . very bad. So here's an ironclad rule for maintaining your self-respect and your sanity: If you find yourself out on a date with an impulsive person who's pressuring you to betray your values, go home and go home fast. Otherwise, before you know it, you'll be in more trouble than you can imagine.

When you feel pressured to do things—or to compromise yourself—in ways that lead you away from God, you're heading straight for major league problems. The best time to decide how you'll behave yourself is before you go out on a date (not during a date!). So don't do the "easy" thing and don't do the impulsive thing. Do the right thing, and do it every time.

—.—.—.—.—.—.—

It wasn't the apple, it was the pair.

Anonymous

WHEN THE BOSS ISN'T WATCHING

Go to the ant, O sluggard. Observe her ways and be wise: which, having no chief, officer or ruler, prepares her food in the summer and gathers her provision in the harvest. How long will you lie down, O sluggard? When will you arise from your sleep?

Proverbs 6:6-9 NASB

The Bible instructs us that we can learn an important lesson from a surprising source: ants. Ants are among nature's most industrious creatures. They do their work without supervision and without hesitation. We should do likewise.

God's Word is clear: We are instructed to work diligently and faithfully. We are told that the fields are ripe for the harvest, that the workers are few, and that the importance of our work is profound. Let us labor, then, for our Master without hesitation and without complaint. Nighttime is coming. Until it does, let us honor our Heavenly Father with grateful hearts and willing hands.

—·—·—·—·—·—

Christian work is any kind of work, from cleaning a sewer to preaching a sermon, that is done by a Christian and offered to God.

Elisabeth Elliot

DEPENDING UPON GOD

Depend on the Lord and his strength; always go to him for help. Remember the miracles he has done; remember his wonders and his decisions.

Psalm 105:4-5 NCV

God's love and support never changes. From the cradle to the grave, God has promised to give you the strength to meet any challenge. God has promised to lift you up and guide your steps if you let Him. God has promised that when you entrust your life to Him completely and without reservation, He will give you the courage to face any trial and the wisdom to live in His righteousness.

God's hand uplifts those who turn their hearts and prayers to Him. Will you count yourself among that number? Will you accept God's peace and wear God's armor against the temptations and distractions of our dangerous world? If you do, you can live courageously and optimistically, knowing that you have been forever touched by the loving, unfailing, uplifting hand of God.

—·—·—·—·—·—·—

God's help is always available, but it is only given to those who seek it.

Max Lucado

SPIRITUAL WEALTH

Trust in your money and down you go! But the godly flourish like leaves in spring.

Proverbs 11:28 NLT

Sometimes it's hard being a Christian, especially when the world keeps pumping out messages that are contrary to your faith.

The media is working around the clock in an attempt to rearrange your priorities. The media says that your appearance is all-important, that your clothes are all-important, that your relationships with the opposite sex are all-important, and that partying is all-important. But guess what? Those messages are lies. The "all-important" things in your life have little to do with parties and appearances. The all-important things in life have to do with your faith, your family, and your future. Period.

Are you willing to stand up for your faith? Are you willing to stand up and be counted, not just in church, where it's relatively easy to be a Christian, but also out there in the "real" world, where it's hard? Hopefully so, because you owe it to God and you owe it to yourself.

—.—.—.—.—.—.—

All those who look to draw their satisfaction from the wells of the world will soon be thirsty again!

Anne Graham Lotz

LAUGHING WITH LIFE

A happy heart makes the face cheerful, but heartache crushes the spirit.

Proverbs 15:13 NIV

Laughter is medicine for the soul, but sometimes, amid the stresses of the day, we forget to take our medicine. Instead of viewing our world with a mixture of optimism and humor, we allow worries and distractions to rob us of the joy that God intends for our lives.

So the next time you find yourself dwelling upon the negatives of life, refocus your attention to things positive. The next time you find yourself falling prey to the blight of pessimism, stop yourself and turn your thoughts around. And, if you see your glass as "half empty," rest assured that your spiritual vision is impaired. With God, your glass is never half empty. With God as your protector and Christ as your Savior, your glass is filled to the brim and overflowing . . . forever.

Today, as you go about your daily activities, approach life with a smile on your lips and hope in your heart. And laugh every chance you get. After all, God created laughter for a reason. So laugh!

—.—.—.—.—.—.—

Laughter is the language of the young at heart and the antidote to what ails us.

Barbara Johnson

WHEN WE DON'T UNDERSTAND

Now we see a dim reflection, as if we were looking into a mirror, but then we shall see clearly. Now I know only a part, but then I will know fully, as God has known me.

1 Corinthians 13:12 NCV

As humans with limited understanding, we can never fully comprehend the hand of God. But as believers in a benevolent God, we must always trust the heart of our Heavenly Father.

Before His crucifixion, Jesus went to the Mount of Olives and poured out His heart to God (Luke 22). Jesus knew of the agony that He was destined to endure, but He also knew that God's will must be done. We, like our Savior, face trials that bring fear and trembling to the very depths of our souls, but like Christ, we, too, must ultimately seek God's will, not our own.

As this day unfolds, seek God's will for your own life and obey His Word. When you entrust your life to Him completely and without reservation, He will give you the strength to meet any challenge, the courage to face any trial, and the wisdom to live in His righteousness and in His peace.

—·—·—·—·—·—·—

A religion that is small enough for our understanding would not be big enough for our needs.

Corrie ten Boom

THE POWER OF PATIENCE

Patience is better than strength. Controlling your temper is better than capturing a city.

Proverbs 16:32 NCV

Temper tantrums are usually unproductive, unattractive, unforgettable, and unnecessary. Perhaps that's why Proverbs 16:32 states that, "Controlling your temper is better than capturing a city."

If you've allowed anger to become a regular visitor at your house, today you must pray for wisdom, for patience, and for a heart that is so filled with love and forgiveness that it contains no room for bitterness. God will help you terminate your tantrums if you ask Him to. And God can help you perfect your ability to be patient if you ask Him to. So ask Him, and then wait patiently for the ever-more-patient you to arrive.

—.—.—.—.—.—.—

When I am dealing with an all-powerful, all-knowing God, I, as a mere mortal, must offer my petitions not only with persistence, but also with patience. Someday I'll know why.

Ruth Bell Graham

INCLUDING GOD IN THE PLANNING PROCESS

There is no wisdom, understanding, or advice that can succeed against the Lord.

Proverbs 21:30 NCV

Does God have a plan for your life? Of course He does! Every day of your life, He is trying to lead you along a path of His choosing . . . but He won't force you to follow. God has given you free will, the opportunity to make decisions for yourself. The choices are yours: either you will choose to obey His Word and seek His will, or you will choose to follow a different path.

Today, as you carve out a few quiet moments to commune with your Heavenly Father, ask Him to renew your sense of purpose. God's plans for you may be far bigger than you imagine, but He may be waiting for you to make the next move—so today, make that move prayerfully, faithfully, and expectantly. And after you've made your move, trust God to make His.

—.—.—.—.—.—.—.—

You can't start building a better tomorrow if you wait till tomorrow to start building.

Marie T. Freeman

WISDOM IS AS WISDOM DOES

A foolish person enjoys doing wrong, but a person with understanding enjoys doing what is wise.

Proverbs 10:23 NCV

Wisdom is not like a mushroom; it does not spring up overnight. It is, instead, like an oak tree that starts as a tiny acorn, grows into a sapling, and eventually reaches up to the sky, tall and strong. To become wise, we must seek God's wisdom and live according to His Word. And, we must not only learn the lessons of the Christian life, we must also live by them.

Do you seek to live a life of righteousness and wisdom? If so, you must study the ultimate source of wisdom: the Word of God. You must seek out worthy mentors and listen carefully to their advice. You must associate, day in and day out, with godly men and women. And, you must act in accordance with your beliefs. When you study God's Word and live according to His commandments, you will become wise . . . and you will be a blessing to your friends, to your family, and to the world.

—.—.—.—.—.—.—

Knowledge can be found in books or in school. Wisdom, on the other hand, starts with God . . . and ends there.

Marie T. Freeman

A NEW LIFE

You have been born again, and this new life did not come from something that dies, but from something that cannot die. You were born again through God's living message that continues forever.

2 Peter 1:23 NCV

God's Word is clear: When we genuinely invite Him to reign over our hearts, and when we accept His transforming love, we are forever changed. When we welcome Christ into our hearts, an old life ends and a new way of living—along with a completely new way of viewing the world—begins.

Each morning offers a fresh opportunity to invite Christ, yet once again, to rule over our hearts and our days. Each morning presents yet another opportunity to take up His cross and follow in His footsteps. Today, let us rejoice in the new life that is ours through Christ, and let us follow Him, step by step, on the path that He first walked.

—.—.—.—.—.—.—

God is not running an antique shop! He is making all things new!

Vance Havner

DREAMS NOT WORTH CHASING

Those who work their land will have plenty of food, but the ones who chase empty dreams instead will end up poor.

Proverbs 28:19 NCV

Some of our most important dreams are the ones we abandon. Some of our most important goals are the ones we don't attain. Sometimes, our most important journeys are the ones that we take to the winding conclusion of what seem to be dead end streets. Thankfully, with God there are no dead ends; there are only opportunities to learn, to yield, to trust, to serve, and to grow.

The next time you experience one of life's inevitable disappointments, don't despair and don't be afraid to try "Plan B." Consider every setback an opportunity to choose a different, more appropriate path. Have faith that God may indeed be leading you in an entirely different direction, a direction of His choosing. And as you take your next step, remember that what looks like a dead end to you may, in fact, be the fast lane according to God.

—.—.—.—.—.—.—

Allow your dreams a place in your prayers and plans. God-given dreams can help you move into the future He is preparing for you.

Barbara Johnson

A LIFETIME OF SPIRITUAL GROWTH

You are God's children whom he loves, so try to be like him. Live a life of love just as Christ loved us and gave himself for us as a sweet-smelling offering and sacrifice to God.

Ephesians 5:1 NCV

The journey toward spiritual maturity lasts a lifetime: As Christians, we can and should continue to grow in the love and the knowledge of our Savior as long as we live. Norman Vincent Peale had simple advice for believers of all ages: "Ask the God who made you to keep remaking you." That advice, of course, is perfectly sound, but too often ignored.

When we cease to grow, either emotionally or spiritually, we do ourselves and our families a profound disservice. But, if we study God's Word, if we obey His commandments, and if we live in the center of His will, we will not be "stagnant" believers; we will, instead, be growing Christians . . . and that's exactly what God wants for our lives.

In those quiet moments when we open our hearts to God, the Creator who made us keeps remaking us. He gives us direction, perspective, wisdom, and courage. And, the appropriate moment to accept His spiritual gifts is always this one.

BEYOND ANXIETY

Anxiety in a man's heart weighs it down, but a good word cheers it up.

Proverbs 12:25 Holman CSB

We live in a world that often breeds anxiety and fear. When we come face to face with tough times, we may fall prey to discouragement, doubt, or depression. But our Father in heaven has other plans. God has promised that we may lead lives of abundance, not anxiety. In fact, His Word instructs us to "be anxious for nothing." But how can we put our fears to rest? By taking those fears to God and leaving them there.

As you face the challenges of everyday living, do you find yourself becoming anxious, troubled, discouraged, or fearful? If so, turn every one of your concerns over to your Heavenly Father. The same God who created the universe will comfort you if you ask Him . . . so ask Him and trust Him. And then watch in amazement as your anxieties melt into the warmth of His loving hands.

—.—.—.—.—.—.—.—

So often we pray and then fret anxiously, waiting for God to hurry up and do something. All the while God is waiting for us to calm down, so He can do something through us.

Corrie ten Boom

NEVER GIVE UP

Even though good people may be bothered by trouble seven times, they are never defeated.

Proverbs 24:16 NCV

In a world filled with roadblocks and stumbling blocks, we need strength, courage, and perseverance. And, as an example of perfect perseverance, we need look no further than our Savior, Jesus Christ.

Jesus finished what He began. Despite the torture He endured, despite the shame of the cross, Jesus was steadfast in His faithfulness to God. We, too, must remain faithful, especially during times of hardship.

Perhaps you are in a hurry for God to reveal His plans for your life. If so, be forewarned: God operates on His own timetable, not yours. Sometimes, God may answer your prayers with silence, and when He does, you must patiently persevere. In times of trouble, you must remain steadfast and trust in the merciful goodness of your Heavenly Father. Whatever your problem, He can handle it. Your job is to keep persevering until He does.

—.—.—.—.—.—.—.—

Don't give up. Moses was once a basket case!

Anonymous

DON'T COMPROMISE

If you're not welcomed, not listened to, quietly withdraw.
Don't make a scene. Shrug your shoulders and be on
your way.

Mark 6:11 MSG

Sometimes, you may feel pressured to compromise yourself, and you may be afraid of what will happen if you firmly say "No." You may be afraid that you'll be rejected. But here's a tip: don't worry too much about rejection, especially when you're rejected for doing the right thing.

Pleasing other people is a good thing . . . up to a point. But you must never allow your "willingness to please" to interfere with your own good judgement or with God's commandments.

Instead of being afraid of rejection, focus on pleasing your Creator first and always. And when it comes to the world and all its inhabitants, don't worry too much about the folks you can't please. Focus, instead, on doing the right thing—and leave the rest up to God.

—.—.—.—.—.—.—

You will get untold flak for prioritizing God's revealed and present will for your life over man's . . . but, boy, is it worth it.

Beth Moore

GUARDING OUR HEARTS AND MINDS

Summing it all up, friends, I'd say you'll do best by filling your minds and meditating on things true, noble, reputable, authentic, compelling, gracious, the best, not the worst; the beautiful, not the ugly; things to praise, not things to curse. Put into practice what you learned from me, what you heard and saw and realized. Do that, and God, who makes everything work together, will work you into his most excellent harmonies.

Philippians 4:8-9 MSG

You are near and dear to God. He loves you more than you can imagine, and He wants the very best for you. And one more thing: God wants you to guard your heart.

Every day, you are faced with choices . . . lots of them. You can do the right thing, or not. You can tell the truth, or not. You can be kind and generous and obedient. Or not.

Your mind and your heart will usually tell you the right thing to do. And if you listen to your parents and grandparents, they will help you, too, by teaching you God's rules. Then, you will learn that doing the right thing is always better than doing the wrong thing. And, by obeying God's rules, you will guard your heart by giving it to His Son Jesus.

UNIQUELY YOU

For you made us only a little lower than God, and you crowned us with glory and honor.

Psalm 8:5 NLT

How many people in the world are exactly like you? The only person in the world who's exactly like you . . . IS YOU! And that means you're special: special to God, special to your family, special to your friends, and a special addition to God's wonderful world!

But sometimes, when you are tired, angry, dejected, or depressed, you may not feel very special. In fact, you may decide that you're the ugliest duckling in the pond, a not-very-special person . . . but whenever you think like that, you're mistaken.

The Bible says that God made you in "an amazing and wonderful way." So the next time that you start feeling like you don't measure up, remember this: when God made all the people of the earth, He only made one you. You're incredibly valuable to God, and that means that you should think of yourself as a V.I.P. (a Very Important Person). God wants you to have the best, and you deserve the best . . . you're worth it!

—.—.—.—.—.—.—

I can tell you, from personal experience of walking with God for over fifty years, that He is the Lover of my soul.

Vonette Bright

WHAT GOD REQUIRES

But he's already made it plain how to live, what to do, what God is looking for in men and women. It's quite simple: Do what is fair and just to your neighbor, be compassionate and loyal in your love, and don't take yourself too seriously—take God seriously.

Micah 6:8 MSG

What does God require of us? That we worship Him only, that we welcome His Son into our hearts, and that we walk humbly with our Creator.

When Jesus was tempted by Satan, the Master's response was unambiguous. Jesus chose to worship the Lord and serve Him only. We, as followers of Christ, must follow in His footsteps.

When we place God in a position of secondary importance, we do ourselves great harm and we put ourselves at great risk. But when we place God squarely in the center of our lives—when we walk humbly and obediently with Him—we are blessed and we are protected.

—.—.—.—.—.—.—

I have discovered that when I please Christ, I end up inadvertently serving others far more effectively.

Beth Moore

THE LOVE OF MONEY . . .

For the love of money is a root of all sorts of evil, and some by longing for it have wandered away from the faith and pierced themselves with many griefs. But flee from these things, you man of God, and pursue righteousness, godliness, faith, love, perseverance and gentleness.

1 Timothy 6:11 NASB

Our society is in love with money and the things that money can buy. God is not. God cares about people, not possessions, and so must we. We must, to the best of our abilities, love our neighbors as ourselves, and we must, to the best of our abilities, resist the mighty temptation to place possessions ahead of people.

Money, in and of itself, is not evil; worshipping money is. So today, as you prioritize your life, remember that God is almighty, but the dollar is not. If we worship God, we are blessed. But if we worship "the almighty dollar," we are inevitably punished because of our misplaced priorities—and our punishment inevitably comes sooner rather than later.

—.—.—.—.—.—.—

When we put people before possessions in our hearts, we are sowing seeds of enduring satisfaction.

Beverly LaHaye

SHARE THE GOOD NEWS

For Christ did not send me to baptize, but to preach the gospel—not with clever words, so that the cross of Christ will not be emptied of its effect.

1 Corinthians 1:17 Holman CSB

A good way to build your faith is by talking about it—and that's precisely what God wants you to do.

In his second letter to Timothy, Paul shares a message to believers of every generation when he writes, "God has not given us a spirit of timidity" (1:7). Paul's meaning is clear: When sharing your testimony, you must be courageous and unashamed.

Let's face facts: You live in a world that desperately needs the healing message of Jesus Christ. Every believer, including you, bears responsibility for sharing the Good News. And it is important to remember that you give your testimony through your words and your actions.

So today, preach the Gospel through your words and your deeds . . . but not necessarily in that order.

—.—.—.—.—.—.—

Claim the joy that is yours. Pray. And know that your joy is used by God to reach others.

Kay Arthur

GODLY THOUGHTS, GODLY ACTIONS

Commit your activities to the Lord and your plans will be achieved.

Proverbs 16:3 Holman CSB

Do you pay careful attention to the quality of your thoughts? And are you careful to direct those thoughts toward topics that are uplifting, enlightening, and pleasing to God? If so, congratulations. But if you find that your thoughts are hijacked from time to time by the negativity that seems to have invaded our troubled world, you are not alone. Ours is a society that focuses on—and often glamorizes—the negative aspects of life, and that's unfortunate.

God intends that you experience joy and abundance. So, today and every day hereafter, celebrate the life that God has given you by focusing your thoughts upon those things that are worthy of praise (Philippians 4:8). And while you're at it, count your blessings instead of your hardships. When you do, you'll undoubtedly offer words of thanks to your Heavenly Father for gifts that are simply too numerous to count.

—·—·—·—·—·—·—

It is the thoughts and intents of the heart that shape a person's life.

John Eldredge

THE POWER OF WILLING HANDS

A lazy person will end up poor, but a hard worker will become rich.

Proverbs 10:4 NCV

God's Word teaches us the value of hard work. In his second letter to the Thessalonians, Paul gives this warning, ". . . if anyone will not work, neither shall he eat" (3:10 NKJV). And the Book of Proverbs proclaims, "A person who doesn't work hard is just like someone who destroys things" (18:9 NCV). In short, God has created a world in which diligence is rewarded but sloth is not. So, whatever it is that you choose to do, do it with enthusiasm and dedication.

Hard work is not simply a proven way to get ahead; it's also part of God's plan for you. God did not create you for a life of mediocrity; He created you for far greater things. Reaching for greater things usually requires work and lots of it, which is perfectly fine with God. After all, He knows that you're up to the task, and He has big plans for you if you possess a loving heart and willing hands.

—.—.—.—.—.—.—.—

I am more and more persuaded that all that is required of us is faithful seed-sowing. The harvest is bound to follow.

Annie Armstrong

FAITHFULNESS AND FOCUS

But if from there you seek the Lord your God, you will find him if you look for him with all your heart and with all your soul.

Deuteronomy 4:29 NIV

God deserves your best. Is He getting it? Do you make an appointment with your Heavenly Father each day? Do you carve out moments when He receives your undivided attention? Or is your devotion to Him fleeting, distracted, and sporadic?

When you acquire the habit of focusing your heart and mind squarely upon God's intentions for your life, He will guide your steps and bless your endeavors. But if you allow distractions to take priority over your relationship with God, they will—and you will pay a price for your mistaken priorities.

Today, focus upon God's Word and upon His will for your life. When you do, you'll be amazed at how quickly everything else comes into focus, too.

—.—.—.—.—.—.—

Jesus challenges you and me to keep our focus daily on the cross of His will if we want to be His disciples.

Anne Graham Lotz

UNDERSTANDING THE GREATNESS OF CHRIST'S LOVE

And I pray that you and all God's holy people will have the power to understand the greatness of Christ's love—how wide and how long and how high and how deep that love is. Christ's love is greater than anyone can ever know, but I pray that you will be able to know that love. Then you can be filled with the fullness of God.

Ephesians 3:18–19 NCV

How much does Christ love us? More than we, as mere mortals, can comprehend. His love is perfect and steadfast. Even though we are fallible and wayward, the Good Shepherd cares for us still. Even though we have fallen far short of the Father's commandments, Christ loves us with a depth that is beyond our understanding. The sacrifice that Jesus made upon the cross was made for each of us, and His love endures to the edge of eternity and beyond.

Christ's love changes everything. When we accept His gift of grace, we are transformed, not only for today, but forever. Yes, Christ's love changes everything. May we invite Him into our hearts so it can then change everything in us.

THE TIME IS NOW

Hard work means prosperity; only fools idle away their time.

Proverbs 12:11 NLT

You can either manage time, or you can waste it. Which kind of person are you: a time manager or a time waster? If you've already learned the importance of managing the clock, then you've discovered how good it feels to get things done when they should be done. But if you've formed the unfortunate habit of having fun first and doing your work second, it's time to think carefully about your priorities.

God created a world in which discipline pays big dividends. And make no mistake: it takes discipline to manage time . . . but it's always worth it. So if you're guilty of wasting more time than you manage, do yourself a favor: get a grip on your life, your clock, and your calendar . . . before it's too late.

—.—.—.—.—.—.—

Life's unfolding stops for no one.

Kathy Troccoli

FAITH ON FIRE

I tell you the truth, whoever believes in me will do the same things that I do. Those who believe will do even greater things than these, because I am going to the Father.

John 14:12 NCV

John Wesley advised, "Catch on fire with enthusiasm and people will come for miles to watch you burn." His words still ring true. When we fan the flames of enthusiasm for Christ, our faith serves as a beacon to others.

Our world desperately needs faithful believers who share the Good News of Jesus with joyful exuberance. Be such a believer. The world desperately needs your enthusiasm, and just as importantly, you need the experience of sharing it.

—.—.—.—.—.—.—

The proper perspective creates within us a spirit of reaching outside of ourselves with joy and enthusiasm.

Luci Swindoll

BEYOND BLAME

When they continued to ask Jesus their question, he raised up and said, "Anyone here who has never sinned can throw the first stone at her."

John 8:7 NCV

To blame others for our own problems is the height of futility. Yet blaming others is a favorite human pastime. Why? Because blaming is much easier than fixing. So instead of solving our problems legitimately (by doing the work required to solve them) we are inclined to fret, to blame, and to criticize, while doing precious little else. When we do, our problems, quite predictably, remain unsolved.

Have you acquired the bad habit of blaming others for problems that you could or should solve yourself? If so, you're wasting precious enegy and precious time. So, as you consider your own situation, remember this: God has a way of helping those who help themselves, but He doesn't spend much time helping those who don't.

—.—.—.—.—.—.—

You'll never win the blame game, so why even bother to play?

Marie T. Freeman

FAIRNESS AND HONEST DEALINGS

The Lord hates dishonest scales, but he is pleased with honest weights.

Proverbs 11:1 NCV

From the time we are children, we are taught that honesty is the best policy, but sometimes, it is so easy to be less than honest. So, we convince ourselves that it's alright to tell "little white lies." But there's a problem: Little white lies tend to grow up, and when they do, they cause havoc and pain in our lives.

For Christians, the issue of honesty is not a topic for debate. Honesty is not just the best policy, it is God's policy, pure and simple. And if we are to be servants worthy of our Savior, Jesus Christ, we should avoid all lies, white or otherwise.

Sometime soon, perhaps even today, you will be tempted to sow the seeds of deception, perhaps in the form of a "harmless" white lie. Resist that temptation. Truth is God's way, and any kind of lie is not.

—.—.—.—.—.—

The single most important element in any human relationship is honesty—with oneself, with God, and with others.

Catherine Marshall

DEFEATING THOSE EVERYDAY FRUSTRATIONS

Foolish people are always fighting, but avoiding quarrels will bring you honor.

Proverbs 20:3 NCV

Anger is a natural human emotion that is sometimes necessary and appropriate. Even Jesus became angry when confronted with the moneychangers in the temple (Matthew 21). Righteous indignation is an appropriate response to evil, but God does not intend that anger should rule our lives. Far from it. God intends that we turn away from anger whenever possible and forgive our neighbors just as we seek forgiveness for ourselves.

Life is full of frustrations: some great and some small. On occasion, you, like Jesus, will confront evil, and when you do, you may respond as He did: vigorously and without reservation. But, more often your frustrations will be of the more mundane variety. As long as you live here on earth, you will face countless opportunities to lose your temper over small, relatively insignificant events: a traffic jam, a spilled cup of coffee, an inconsiderate comment, a broken promise. When you are tempted to lose your temper over the minor inconveniences of life, don't. Turn away from anger, hatred, bitterness, and regret. Turn instead to God. When you do, you'll be following His commandments and giving yourself a priceless gift . . . the gift of peace.

ENOUGH IS ENOUGH

Let your character be free from the love of money, being content with what you have; for He Himself has said, "I will never desert you, nor will I ever forsake you."

Hebrews 13:5 NASB

Ours is a world that glorifies material possessions. Christians, of course, should not. As believers who have been touched and transformed by the grace of a risen Savior, we must never allow the things of this earth to distance us from our sense of God's presence and the direction of God's hand. If we are to enjoy the peace and abundance that God has promised us, we must reign in our desire for more and more; we must acknowledge that when it comes to earthly possessions, enough is always enough.

—.—.—.—.—.—.—

Yes, we were created for His holy pleasure, but we will ultimately—if not immediately—find much pleasure in His pleasure.

Beth Moore

PURPOSE THROUGH SERVICE

But he who is greatest among you shall be your servant. And whoever exalts himself will be humbled, and he who humbles himself will be exalted.

Matthew 23:11-12 NLT

The words of Jesus are clear: the most esteemed men and women in this world are not the big-shots who jump up on stage and hog the spotlight; the greatest among us are those who are willing to become humble servants.

Are you willing to become a servant for Christ? Are you willing to pitch in and make the world a better place, or are you determined to keep all your blessings to yourself? Hopefully, you are determined to follow Christ's example by making yourself an unselfish servant to those who need your help.

Today, you may be tempted to take more than you give. But if you feel the urge to be selfish, resist that urge with all your might. Don't be stingy, selfish, or self-absorbed. Instead, serve your friends quietly and without fanfare. Find a need and fill it . . . humbly. Lend a helping hand . . . anonymously. Share a word of kindness . . . with quiet sincerity. As you go about your daily activities, remember that the Savior of all humanity made Himself a servant, and we, as His followers, must do no less.

HE RESTORES YOUR STRENGTH

Do not remember the past events, pay no attention to things of old. Look, I am about to do something new; even now it is coming. Do you not see it? Indeed, I will make a way in the wilderness, rivers in the desert.

Isaiah 43:18-19 Holman CSB

For an extremely busy girl living in an extremely busy world, life may seem like a merry-go-round that never stops turning. If that description fits you, then you may find yourself running short of patience or strength, or both. If you're feeling exhausted or discouraged, there is a source from which you can draw the power needed to recharge your spiritual batteries. That source is God.

Have you "tapped in" to the power of God? Have you turned your life and your heart over to Him, or are you muddling along under your own power? The answers to these questions will determine the quality of your life here on earth and the destiny of your life throughout all eternity.

Do you feel like your emotional resources are almost gone? Call upon fellow believers to support you, and call upon Christ to renew your spirit and your life. When you do, you'll discover that the Creator of the universe can make everything new, including you.

LOVING GOD AND OTHERS

Jesus replied, "'Love the Lord your God with all your heart and with all your soul and with all your mind.' This is the first and greatest commandment. And the second is like it: 'Love your neighbor as yourself.' All the Law and the Prophets hang on these two commandments."

Matthew 22:37-40 NIV

Christ's words leave no room for interpretation: He instructs us to love the Lord with all our hearts and to love our neighbors as we love ourselves. But sometimes, despite our best intentions, we fall short. When we become embittered with ourselves, with our neighbors, or most especially with God, we disobey the One who gave His life for us. And we bring inevitable, needless suffering into our lives.

If we are to please God, we must cleanse ourselves of the negative feelings that separate us from others and from Him. In 1 Corinthians 13, we are told that love is the foundation upon which all our relationships are to be built—our relationships with others and our relationship with our Creator. May we fill our hearts with love; may we never yield to bitterness. And may we praise the Son of God who, in His infinite wisdom, made love His greatest commandment.

WORSHIPPING THE RISEN CHRIST

He is not here, but He has been resurrected!

Luke 24:6 Holman CSB

God has a wonderful plan for your life, and an important part of that plan includes worship. We should never deceive ourselves: every life is based upon some form of worship. The question is not whether we worship, but what we worship.

Some of us choose to worship God. The result is a plentiful harvest of joy, peace, and abundance. Others distance themselves from God by foolishly worshiping earthly possessions and personal gratification. To do so is a mistake of profound proportions.

Have you accepted the grace of God's only begotten Son? Then worship Him. Worship Him today and every day. Worship Him with sincerity and thanksgiving. Write His name on your heart and rest assured that He, too, has written your name on His.

—.—.—.—.—.—.—.—

When we are in a situation where Jesus is all we have, we soon discover he is all we really need.

Gigi Graham Tchividjian

NEW BEGINNINGS

Give your entire attention to what God is doing right now, and don't get worked up about what may or may not happen tomorrow. God will help you deal with whatever hard things come up when the time comes.

Matthew 6:34 MSG

Today, like every other day, is literally brimming with possibilities. Whether we realize it or not, God is always working in us and through us; our job is to let Him do His work without undo interference. Yet we are imperfect beings who, because of limited vision, often resist God's will. We want life to unfold according to our own desires, not God's. But our Heavenly Father may have other plans.

As you begin the new year, think carefully about the work that God can do through you. And then, welcome the coming year with a renewed sense of purpose and hope. God has the power to make all things new, including you. Your task is to let Him do it.

—.—.—.—.—.—.—

Commitment to His lordship on Easter, at revivals, or even every Sunday is not enough. We must choose this day—and every day—whom we will serve. This deliberate act of the will is the inevitable choice between habitual fellowship and habitual failure.

Beth Moore

FIRST THINGS FIRST

Happy is the person who finds wisdom, the one who gets understanding.

Proverbs 3:13 NCV

When something important needs to be done, the best time to do it is sooner rather than later. But sometimes, instead of doing the smart thing (which, by the way, is choosing "sooner"), we may choose "later." When we do, we may pay a heavy price for our shortsightedness.

Are you one of those people who puts things off till the last minute? If so, it's time to change your ways. Your procrastination is probably the result of your shortsighted attempt to postpone (or avoid altogether) the discomfort that you associate with a particular activity. Get over it!

Whatever "it" is, do it now. When you do, you won't have to worry about "it" later.

—·—·—·—·—·—·—

Today is mine. Tomorrow is none of my business. If I peer anxiously into the fog of the future, I will strain my spiritual eyes so that I will not see clearly what is required of me now.

Elisabeth Elliot

ON GUARD AGAINST EVIL

Your love must be real. Hate what is evil, and hold on to what is good.

Romans 12:9 NCV

Face facts: this world is inhabited by quite a few people who are very determined to do evil things. The devil and his human helpers are working 24/7 to cause pain and heartbreak in every corner of the globe . . . including your corner. So you'd better beware.

Your job, if you choose to accept it, is to recognize evil and fight it. The moment that you decide to fight evil whenever you see it, you can no longer be a lukewarm, halfhearted Christian. And, when you are no longer a lukewarm Christian, God rejoices while the devil despairs.

When will you choose to get serious about fighting the evils of our world? Before you answer that question, consider this: in the battle of good versus evil, the devil never takes a day off . . . and neither should you.

—·—·—·—·—·—·—

I can still hardly believe it. I, with shriveled, bent fingers, atrophied muscles, gnarled knees, and no feeling from the shoulders down, will one day have a new body—light, bright and clothed in righteousness—powerful and dazzling.

Joni Eareckson Tada

IN SEARCH OF A QUIET CONSCIENCE

My son, if sinners entice you, don't be persuaded.

Proverbs 1:10 Holman CSB

A clear conscience is one of the many rewards you earn when you obey God's Word and follow His will. Whenever you know that you've done the right thing, you feel better about yourself, your life, and your future. A guilty conscience, on the other hand, is, for most people, it's own punishment.

In order to keep your conscience clear, you should study God's Word and obey it—you should seek God's will and follow it—you should honor God's Son and walk with Him. When you do, your earthly rewards are never-ceasing, and your heavenly rewards are everlasting.

—.—.—.—.—.—.—

God desires that we become spiritually healthy enough through faith to have a conscience that rightly interprets the work of the Holy Spirit.

Beth Moore

THE PROBLEM OF SIN

Watch and pray so that you will not fall into temptation. The spirit is willing but the body is weak.

Matthew 26:41 NIV

After fasting forty days and nights in the desert, Jesus was tempted by Satan. Christ used Scripture to rebuke the devil (Matthew 4:1-11). We must do likewise. The Holy Bible provides us with a perfect blueprint for righteous living. If we consult that blueprint daily and follow it carefully, we build our lives according to God's plan.

We live in a world that is brimming with opportunities to stray from God's will. Ours is a society filled with temptations, a place where it is all too easy to disobey God. We, like our Savior, must guard ourselves against these temptations. We do so, in part, through prayer and through a careful reading of God's Word.

The battle against Satan is ongoing. Be vigilant, and call upon God to protect you. When you petition Him with a sincere heart, God will be your shield, always.

—.—.—.—.—.—.—.—

There is sharp necessity for giving Christ absolute obedience. The devil bids for our complete self-will. To whatever extent we give this self-will the right to be master over our lives, we are, to an extent, giving Satan a toehold.

Catherine Marshall

YOUR TO-DO LIST . . . AND GOD'S

Draw near to God, and He will draw near to you.

James 4:8 Holman CSB

Have you fervently asked God to help prioritize your life? Have you asked Him for guidance and for the courage to do the things that you know need to be done? If so, then you're continually inviting your Creator to reveal Himself in a variety of ways. As a follower of Christ, you must do no less.

When you make God's priorities your priorities, you will receive God's abundance and His peace. When you make God a full partner in every aspect of your life, He will lead you along the proper path: His path. When you allow God to reign over your heart, He will honor you with spiritual blessings that are simply too numerous to count. So, as you plan for the day ahead, make God's will your ultimate priority. When you do, every other priority will have a tendency to fall neatly into place.

—.—.—.—.—.—.—.—

With God, it's never "Plan B" or "second best." It's always "Plan A." And, if we let Him, He'll make something beautiful of our lives.

Gloria Gaither

FINDING COMFORT

I was very worried, but you comforted me . . . .

Psalm 94:19 NCV

If you are a person with lots of obligations and plenty of responsibilities, it is simply a fact of life: You worry. From time to time, you worry about health, about money, about safety, about family, and about countless other concerns, some great and some small.

Where is the best place to take your worries? Take them to God. Take your troubles to Him; take your fears to Him; take your doubts to Him; take your weaknesses to Him; take your sorrows to Him . . . and leave them all there. Seek protection from the One who offers you eternal salvation; build your spiritual house upon the Rock that cannot be moved.

—.—.—.—.—.—.—

God is great; God is good; God loves you, and He sent His Son to die for your sins. When you keep these things in mind, you'll discover that it's hard to stay worried for long.

Marie T. Freeman

GOD CARES

For the Lord your God is the God of gods and Lord of lords, the great, mighty, and awesome God.

Deuteronomy 10:17 Holman CSB

It's a promise that is made over and over again in the Bible: Whatever "it" is, God can handle it.

Life isn't always easy. Far from it! Sometimes, life can be very, very tough. But even then, even during our darkest moments, we're protected by a loving Heavenly Father. When we're worried, God can reassure us; when we're sad, God can comfort us. When our hearts are broken, God is not just near; He is here. So we must lift our thoughts and prayers to Him. When we do, He will answer our prayers. Why? Because He is our Shepherd, and He has promised to protect us now and forever.

—.—.—.—.—.—.—

The God who created and numbers the stars in the heavens also numbers the hairs of my head. He pays attention to very big things and to very small ones. What matters to me matters to Him, and that changes my life.

Elisabeth Elliot

THE WISDOM OF KINDNESS

Kind people do themselves a favor, but cruel people bring trouble on themselves.

Proverbs 11:17 NCV

Christ showed His love for us by willingly sacrificing His own life so that we might have eternal life: "But God demonstrates his own love for us in this: While we were still sinners, Christ died for us" (Romans 5:8 NIV). We, as Christ's followers, are challenged to share His love with kind words on our lips and praise in our hearts.

Just as Christ has been—and will always be—the ultimate friend to His flock, so should we be Christlike in the kindness and generosity that we show toward others, especially those who are most in need.

When we walk each day with Jesus—and obey the commandments found in God's Holy Word—we become worthy ambassadors for Christ. When we share the love of Christ, we share a priceless gift with the world. As His servants, we must do no less.

—.—.—.—.—.—.—

Be so preoccupied with good will that you haven't room for ill will.

E. Stanley Jones

CLAIMING CONTENTMENT IN A DISCONTENTED WORLD

Serving God does make us very rich, if we are satisfied with what we have.

1 Timothy 6:6 NCV

The preoccupation with happiness and contentment is an ever-present theme in the modern world. We are bombarded with messages that tell us where to find peace and pleasure in a world that worships materialism and wealth. But, lasting contentment is not found in material possessions; genuine contentment is a spiritual gift from God to those who trust in Him and follow His commandments.

Where do we find contentment? If we don't find it in God, we will never find it anywhere else. But, if we put our faith and our trust in Him, we will be blessed with an inner peace that is beyond human understanding. When God dwells at the center of our lives, peace and contentment will belong to us just as surely as we belong to God.

—.—.—.—.—.—.—

When we do what is right, we have contentment, peace, and happiness.

Beverly LaHaye

OBEDIENCE AND PRAISE

Praise the Lord! Happy are those who respect the Lord, who want what he commands.

Psalm 112:1 NCV

Oswald Chambers, the author of the Christian classic devotional text, *My Utmost For His Highest*, advised, "Never support an experience which does not have God as its source, and faith in God as its result." These words serve as a powerful reminder that, as Christians, we are called to walk with God and obey His commandments. God gave us His commandments for a reason: so that we might obey them and be blessed.

We live in a world that presents us with countless temptations to stray far from God's path. But, when confronted with sin, we Christians have clear instructions: Walk—or better yet run—in the opposite direction.

—.—.—.—.—.—.—

Obey God one step at a time, then the next step will come into view.

Catherine Marshall

THE HEALING TOUCH OF THE MASTER'S HAND

Those who sow in tears shall reap in joy.

Psalm 126:5 NKJV

Grief visits all of us who live long and love deeply. When we lose a loved one, or when we experience any other profound loss, darkness overwhelms us for a while, and it seems as if we cannot summon the strength to face another day—but, with God's help, we can.

When our friends or family members encounter life-shattering events, we struggle to find words that might offer them comfort and support. But finding the right words can be difficult, if not impossible. Sometimes, all we can do is to be with our loved ones, offering them few words but much love.

Thankfully, God promises that He is "near to those who have a broken heart" (Psalm 34:18 NKJV). In times of intense sadness, we must turn to Him, and we must encourage our friends and family members to do likewise. When we do, our Father comforts us and, in time, He heals us.

—.—.—.—.—.—.—

When we cry, we allow our bodies to function according to God's design—and we embrace one of the "perks" he offers to relieve our stress.

Barbara Johnson

WALKING IN THE LIGHT

I am the light of the world. Whoever follows me will never walk in darkness, but will have the light of life.

John 8:12 NIV

God's Word instructs us that Jesus is, "the way, the truth, and the life" (John 14:6-7). Without Christ, we are as far removed from salvation as the east is removed from the west. And without Christ, we can never know the ultimate truth: God's truth.

Truth is God's way: He commands His believers to live in truth, and He rewards those who do so. Jesus is the personification of God's liberating truth, a truth that offers salvation to mankind.

Do you seek to walk with God? Do you seek to feel His presence and His peace? Then you must walk in truth; you must walk in the light; you must walk with the Savior. There is simply no other way.

—.—.—.—.—.—.—

God will see to it that we understand as much truth as we are willing to obey.

Elisabeth Elliot

PROSPEROUS GENEROSITY

The one who blesses others is abundantly blessed; those who help others are helped.

Proverbs 11:25 MSG

God's Word commands us to be generous, compassionate servants to those who need our support. As believers, we have been richly blessed by our Creator. We, in turn, are called to share our gifts, our possessions, our testimonies, and our talents.

Concentration camp survivor Corrie ten Boom correctly observed, "The measure of a life is not its duration but its donation." These words remind us that the quality of our lives is determined not by what we are able to take from others, but instead by what we are able to share with others.

The thread of generosity is woven into the very fabric of Christ's teachings. If we are to be disciples of Christ, we, too, must be cheerful, generous, courageous givers. Our Savior expects no less from us. And He deserves no less.

—.—.—.—.—.—.—.—

What is your focus today? Joy comes when it is Jesus first, others second . . . then you.

Kay Arthur

A STEADFAST FAITH IN A STEADFAST GOD

I have set the Lord always before me; because He is at my right hand I shall not be moved.

Psalm 16:8 NKJV

God is faithful to us even when we are not faithful to Him. God keeps His promises to us even when we stray far from His will. He continues to love us even when we disobey His commandments. But God does not force His blessings upon us. If we are to experience His love and His grace, we must claim them for ourselves.

Are you tired, discouraged, or fearful? Be comforted: God is with you. Are you confused? Listen to the quiet voice of your Heavenly Father. Are you bitter? Talk with God and seek His guidance. Are you celebrating a great victory? Thank God and praise Him. He is the Giver of all things good.

In whatever condition you find yourself, wherever you are, whether you are happy or sad, victorious or vanquished, troubled or triumphant, remember that God is faithful and that His love is eternal. And be comforted. God is not just near. He is here.

USING YOUR GIFTS TO SERVE

There are different kinds of gifts, but they are all from the same Spirit. There are different ways to serve but the same Lord to serve.

1 Corinthians 12:4–5 NCV

God gives each of us a unique assortment of talents and opportunities. And our Heavenly Father instructs us to be faithful stewards of the gifts that He bestows upon us. But we live in a world that encourages us to do otherwise.

Ours is a society that is filled to the brim with countless opportunities to squander our time, our resources, and our talents. So we must be watchful for distractions and temptations that might lead us astray.

God has blessed you with unique opportunities to serve Him, and He has given you every tool that you need to do so. Today, accept this challenge: value the talent that God has given you, nourish it, make it grow, and share it with the world. After all, the best way to say "Thank You" for God's gifts is to use them.

—.—.—.—.—.—

Doing something positive toward another person is a practical approach to feeling good about yourself.

Barbara Johnson

FORGIVENESS IS A FORM OF WISDOM

The discretion of a man makes him slow to anger, and his glory is to overlook a transgression.

Proverbs 19:11 NCV

Bitterness is a form of self-punishment; forgiveness is a means of self-liberation. Bitterness focuses on the injustices of the past; forgiveness focuses on the blessings of the present and the opportunities of the future. Bitterness is an emotion that destroys you; forgiveness is a decision that empowers you. Bitterness is folly; forgiveness is wisdom.

Sometimes, amid the demands of daily life, we lose perspective. Life seems out of balance, and the pressures of everyday living seem overwhelming. What's needed is a fresh perspective, a restored sense of balance . . . and God's wisdom.

If we call upon the Lord and seek to see the world through His eyes, He will give us guidance, wisdom and perspective. When we make God's priorities our priorities, He will lead us according to His plan and according to His commandments. When we study God's Word, we are reminded that God's reality is the ultimate reality. May we live—and forgive—accordingly.

CELEBRATING GOD'S HANDIWORK

The heavens declare the glory of God, and the sky proclaims the work of His hands.

Psalm 19:1 Holman CSB

When we slow down long enough to think about—and pay careful attention to—God's glorious universe, we marvel at the miracle of nature. The smallest seedlings and grandest stars are all part of God's infinite creation. God has placed His handiwork on display for all to see, and if we are wise, we will take time each day to celebrate the world that surrounds us.

Today, as you fulfill the demands of everyday life, pause to consider the majesty of heaven and earth. It is as miraculous as it is beautiful, as incomprehensible as it is breathtaking.

The Psalmist reminds us that the heavens are a declaration of God's glory. May we never cease to praise the Father for a universe that stands as an awesome testimony to His presence and His power.

—.—.—.—.—.—.—

It is impossible for me to look at the heavens at night without realizing there had to be a Creator.

Ruth Bell Graham

THE MIGHTY WORKS OF THOSE WHO BELIEVE

Most assuredly, I say to you, he who believes in Me, the works that I do he will do also.

John 14:12 NKJV

The central message of James' letter is the need for believers to act upon their beliefs. James' instruction is clear: "faith without works is dead." We are saved by our faith in Christ, but salvation does not signal the end of our earthly responsibilities; it marks the true beginning of our work for the Lord.

If your faith in God is strong, you will find yourself drawn toward God's work. You will serve Him, not just with words or prayers, but also with deeds. Because of your faith, you will feel compelled to do God's work—to do it gladly, faithfully, joyfully, and consistently.

Today, redouble your efforts to do God's bidding here on earth. Never have the needs—or the opportunities—been greater.

—.— A TIP —.—

In the fulfillment of your duties, let your intentions be so pure that you reject from your actions any other motive than the glory of God and the salvation of souls.

WALKING WITH THE WISE

Whoever walks with the wise will become wise; whoever walks with fools will suffer harm.

Proverbs 13:20 NLT

Do you want to become wise? Then you must walk with people who, by their words and their presence, make you wiser. And, to the best of your ability, you must avoid those people who encourage you to think foolish thoughts or do foolish things.

Today, as a gift to yourself, select, from your friends and family members, a mentor whose judgement you trust. Then listen carefully to your mentor's advice and be willing to accept that advice, even if accepting it requires effort or pain, or both. Consider your mentor to be God's gift to you. Thank God for that gift, and use it.

—.—.—.—.—.—.—

When you and I are related to Jesus Christ, our strength and wisdom and peace and joy and love and hope may run out, but His life rushes in to keep us filled to the brim. We are showered with blessings, not because of anything we have or have not done, but simply because of Him.

Anne Graham Lotz

DAILY DISTRACTIONS

Don't worry about your life, what you will eat or what you will drink; or about your body, what you will wear. Isn't life more than food and the body more than clothing?

Matthew 6:25 Holman CSB

All of us must live through those days when the traffic jams, the computer crashes, and the dog makes a main course out of our homework. But, when we find ourselves distracted by the minor frustrations of life, we must catch ourselves, take a deep breath, and lift our thoughts upward.

Although we may, at times, struggle mightily to rise above the distractions of everyday living, we need never struggle alone. God is here—eternal and faithful, with infinite patience and love—and, if we reach out to Him, He will restore our sense of perspective and give peace to our souls.

—.—.—.—.—.—.—

O Lord, thank You that Your side of the embroidery of our life is always perfect. That is such a comfort when our side is sometimes so mixed up.

Corrie ten Boom

A FUTURE SO BRIGHT . . .

Wisdom is pleasing to you. If you find it, you have hope for the future.

Proverbs 24:14 NCV

Let's talk for a minute about the future . . . your future. How bright do you believe your future to be? Well, if you're a faithful believer, God has plans for you that are so bright that you'd better pack several pairs of sunglasses and a lifetime supply of sunblock!

The way that you think about your future will play a powerful role in determining how things turn out (it's called the "self-fulfilling prophecy," and it applies to everybody, including you). So here's another question: Are you expecting a terrific tomorrow, or are you dreading a terrible one? The answer to that question will have a powerful impact on the way tomorrow unfolds.

Today, as you live in the present and look to the future, remember that God has an amazing plan for you. Act—and believe—accordingly. And one more thing: don't forget the sunblock.

—.—.—.—.—.—

Never be afraid to trust an unknown future to a known God.

Corrie ten Boom

WHEN GOD SPEAKS QUIETLY

Speak, Lord. I am your servant and I am listening.

1 Samuel 3:10 NCV

Sometimes God speaks loudly and clearly. More often, He speaks in a quiet voice—and if you are wise, you will be listening carefully when He does. To do so, you must carve out quiet moments each day to study His Word and sense His direction.

Can you quiet yourself long enough to listen to your conscience? Are you attuned to the subtle guidance of your intuition? Are you willing to pray sincerely and then wait quietly for God's response. Hopefully so. Usually God refrains from sending His messages on stone tablets or city billboards. More often, He communicates in more subtle ways. If you sincerely desire to hear His voice, you must listen carefully, and you must do so in the silent corners of your quiet, willing heart.

—.—.—.—.—.—.—

It is in that stillness that the Voice will be heard, the only voice in all the universe that speaks peace to the deepest part of us.

Elisabeth Elliot

RIGHTEOUSNESS AND RIGHTNESS

Christ ended the law so that everyone who believes in him may be right with God.

Romans 10:4 NCV

How do we live a life that is "right with God"? By accepting God's Son and obeying His commandments. Accepting Christ is a decision that we make one time; following in His footsteps requires thousands of decisions each day.

Whose steps will you follow today? Will you honor God as you strive to follow His Son? Or will you join the lockstep legion that seeks to discover happiness and fulfillment through worldly means? If you are righteous and wise, you will follow Christ. You will follow Him today and every day. You will seek to walk in His footsteps without reservation or doubt. When you do so, you will be "right with God" precisely because you are walking aright with His only begotten Son.

—.—.—.—.—.—.—.—

There was One, who for "us sinners and our salvation," left the glories of heaven and sojourned upon this earth in weariness and woe, amid those who hated his and finally took his life.

Lottie Moon

HOPE NOW!

Delayed hope makes the heart sick.

Proverbs 13:12 Holman CSB

The hope that the world offers is fleeting and imperfect. The hope that God offers is unchanging, unshakable, and unending. It is no wonder, then, that when we seek security from worldly sources, our hopes are often dashed. Thankfully, God has no such record of failure.

Where will you place your hopes today? Will you entrust your future to man or to God? Will you seek solace exclusively from fallible human beings, or will you place your hopes, first and foremost, in the trusting hands of your Creator? The decision is yours, and you must live with the results of the choice you make.

For thoughtful believers, hope begins with God. Period. So today, as you embark upon the next stage of your life's journey, consider the words of the Psalmist: "You are my hope; O Lord GOD, You are my confidence" (71:5 NASB). Then, place your trust in the One who cannot be shaken.

—.—.—.—.—.—.—

God is the only one who can make the valley of trouble a door of hope.

Catherine Marshall

HE'S NUMBER ONE

Do not have other gods besides Me.

Exodus 20:3 Holman CSB

Who is in charge of your heart? Is it God, or is it something else? Have you given Christ your heart, your soul, your talents, your time, and your testimony? Or are you giving Him little more than a few hours each Sunday morning?

In the book of Exodus, God warns that we should place no gods before Him. Yet all too often, we place our Lord in second, third, or fourth place as we worship other things. When we unwittingly place possessions or relationships above our love for the Creator, we create big problems for ourselves.

Does God rule your heart? Make certain that the honest answer to this question is a resounding yes. In the life of every radical believer, God comes first. And that's precisely the place that He deserves in your heart.

—.—.—.—.—.—.—.—

Give God what's right—not what's left!

Anonymous

BEING TRUE TO YOURSELF . . . AND TO GOD

The righteous man leads a blameless life; blessed are his children after him.

Proverbs 20:7 NIV

Charles Swindoll correctly observed, "Nothing speaks louder or more powerfully than a life of integrity." Godly girls agree.

Integrity is built slowly over a lifetime. It is a precious thing—difficult to build but easy to tear down. As believers in Christ, we must seek to live each day with discipline, honesty, and faith. When we do, at least two things happen: integrity becomes a habit, and God blesses us because of our obedience to Him.

Living a life of integrity isn't always the easiest way, but it is always the right way. And God clearly intends that it should be our way, too.

—.—.—.—.—.—.—

Just pray for a tough hide and a tender heart.

Ruth Bell Graham

THE FUTILITY OF FOOLISH ARGUMENTS

But stay away from those who have foolish arguments and talk about useless family histories and argue and quarrel about the law. Those things are worth nothing and will not help anyone.

Titus 3:9 NCV

Arguments are seldom won but often lost. When we engage in petty squabbles, our losses usually outpace our gains. When we acquire the unfortunate habit of habitual bickering, we do harm to our friends, to our families, to our coworkers, and to ourselves.

Time and again, God's Word warns us that most arguments are a monumental waste of time, of energy, and of life. In Titus, we are warned to refrain from "foolish arguments," and with good reason. Such arguments usually do more for the devil than they do for God.

So the next time you're tempted to engage in a silly squabble, whether inside the church or outside it, refrain. When you do, you'll put a smile on God's face, and you'll send the devil packing.

—·—·—·—·—·—

God loves everyone, but probably prefers "fruits of the spirit" over "religious nuts"!

Anonymous

DUTY TO GOD AND MANKIND

His master replied, "Well done, good and faithful servant! You have been faithful with a few things; I will put you in charge of many things. Come and share your master's happiness!"

Matthew 25:21 NIV

God has promised us this: when we do our duties in small matters, He will give us additional responsibilities. When we do our work dutifully, and when we behave responsibly, God rewards us—in a time and in a manner of His choosing, not our own.

Sometimes, God rewards us by giving us additional burdens to bear, or by changing the course of our lives so that we may better serve Him. Sometimes, our rewards come in the form of temporary setbacks that lead, in turn, to greater victories. Sometimes, God rewards us by answering "no" to our prayers so that He can say "yes" to a far grander request that we, with our limited understanding, would never have thought to ask for.

If you seek to be God's servant in great matters, be faithful, be patient, and be dutiful in smaller matters. Then step back and watch as God surprises you with the spectacular creativity of His infinite wisdom and His perfect plan.

A THIRST FOR GOD

My soul thirsts for God, for the living God.

Psalm 42:2 NKJV

Where is God? He is everywhere you have ever been and everywhere you will ever go. He is with you throughout the night and all through the day; He knows your every thought; He hears your every heartbeat.

When you earnestly seek Him, you will find Him because He is here, waiting patiently for you to reach out to Him . . . right here . . . right now. And make no mistake: your soul does indeed thirst for God. That thirst is planted in your heart, and it is a thirst that only God can quench. Let Him. . . right here . . . right now.

—.—.—.—.—.—.—

One of the most wonderful things about knowing God is that there's always so much more to know, so much more to discover. Just when we least expect it, He intrudes into our neat and tidy notions about who He is and how He works.

Joni Eareckson Tada

WITH CHRISTLIKE HUMILITY

Make your own attitude that of Christ Jesus.

Philippians 2:5 Holman CSB

Dietrich Bonhoeffer observed, "It is very easy to overestimate the importance of our own achievements in comparison with what we owe others." How true. Even those of us who consider ourselves "self-made" men and women are deeply indebted to more people than we can count. Our first and greatest indebtedness, of course, is to God and His only begotten Son. But we are also indebted to ancestors, parents, teachers, friends, spouses, family members, coworkers, fellow believers and the list goes on.

With so many people who rightfully deserve to share the credit for our successes, how can we gloat? The answer, of course, is that we should not. Proverbs 16:18 warns us that "Pride goes before destruction . . ." (NIV). And 1 Peter 5:5 teaches us that "God opposes the proud but gives grace to the humble" (NIV).

You are entitled to take pride in your accomplishments. But not too much pride. Instead of puffing out your chest and saying, "Look at me!", give credit where credit is due, starting with God. And rest assured: There is no such thing as a self-made man. All of us are made by God . . . and He deserves the glory, not us.

LIVING SIMPLY IN A COMPLICATED WORLD

Do not conform any longer to the pattern of this world, but be transformed by the renewing of your mind. Then you will be able to test and approve what God's will is—his good, pleasing and perfect will.

Romans 12:2 NIV

Is yours a life of moderation or accumulation? Are you more interested in the possessions you can acquire or in the person you can become? The answers to these questions will determine the direction of your day and, in time, the direction of your life.

Ours is a highly complicated society, a place where people and corporations vie for your attention, for your time, and for your dollars. Don't let them succeed in complicating your life! Keep your eyes focused instead upon God.

If your material possessions are somehow distancing you from God, discard them. If your outside interests leave you too little time for your family or your God, slow down the merry-go-round or, better yet, get off completely. Remember: God wants your full attention, and He wants it today, so don't let anybody or anything get in His way.

CHEERFUL CHRISTIANITY

The cheerful heart has a continual feast.

Proverbs 15:15 NIV

Few things in life are more sad, or, for that matter, more absurd, than a grumpy Christian. Christ promises us lives of abundance and joy, but He does not force His joy upon us. We must claim His joy for ourselves, and when we do, Jesus, in turn, fills our spirits with His power and His love.

How can we receive from Christ the joy that is rightfully ours? By giving Him what is rightfully His: our hearts and our souls.

When we earnestly commit ourselves to the Savior of mankind, when we place Jesus at the center of our lives and trust Him as our personal Savior, He will transform us, not just for today, but for all eternity. Then we, as God's children, can share Christ's joy and His message with a world that needs both.

—.—.—.—.—.—.—

God is good, and heaven is forever. And if those two facts don't cheer you up, nothing will.

Marie T. Freeman

REMEMBERING GOD'S LOVE

For the Lord is good; His mercy is everlasting, and His truth endures to all generations.

Psalm 100:5 NKJV

How much does God love you? As long as you're alive, you'll never be able to figure it out because God's love is just too big to comprehend. But this much we know: God loves you so much that He sent His Son Jesus to come to this earth and to die for you! And, when you accepted Jesus into your heart, God gave you a gift that is more precious than gold: the gift of eternal life.

God's love is bigger and more powerful than anybody can imagine, but His love is very real. So do yourself a favor right now: accept God's love with open arms and welcome His Son Jesus into your heart. When you do, your life will be changed today, tomorrow, and forever.

—.—.—.—.—.—.—.—

The unfolding of our friendship with the Father will be a never-ending revelation stretching on into eternity.

Catherine Marshall

THE IMPORTANCE OF WORDS

So then, rid yourselves of all evil, all lying, hypocrisy, jealousy, and evil speech. As newborn babies want milk, you should want the pure and simple teaching. By it you can grow up and be saved.

1 Peter 2:1–2 NCV

How important are the words we speak? More important than we realize. Our words have echoes that extend beyond place or time. If our words are encouraging, we can lift others up; if our words are hurtful, we can hold others back.

Do you seek to be a source of encouragement to others? And, do you seek to be a worthy ambassador for Christ? If so, you must speak words that are worthy of your Savior. So avoid angry outbursts. Refrain from impulsive outpourings. Terminate tantrums. Instead, speak words of encouragement and hope to your family and friends, who, by the way, most certainly need all the hope and encouragement they can find.

—.—.—.—.—.—.—

Words. Do you fully understand their power? Can any of us really grasp the mighty force behind the things we say? Do we stop and think before we speak, considering the potency of the words we utter?

Joni Eareckson Tada

MAKING THE MOST OF WHATEVER COMES

A man's heart plans his way, but the Lord determines his steps.

Proverbs 16:9 Holman CSB

As each day unfolds, we are literally surrounded by more opportunities than we can count—opportunities to improve our own lives and the lives of those we love. Each of us possesses the ability to experience earthly peace and spiritual abundance, but sometimes peace and abundance seem to be little more than distant promises.

As we face the challenges that are part of life here on earth, we must not become discouraged. We must instead arm ourselves with the promises of God. When we do, we can expect the very best that life—and God—has to offer.

Do you expect the coming day to be a fountain of opportunities? Are you expecting the best (and preparing yourself for it), or are you expecting the worst (and bracing yourself against it)? The answer to these questions will have a profound and surprising influence on the quality of your day and your life.

OUR ACTIONS REVEAL OUR BELIEFS

Therefore by their fruits you will know them.

Matthew 7:20 NKJV

English clergyman Thomas Fuller observed, "He does not believe who does not live according to his beliefs." These words are most certainly true. We may proclaim our beliefs to our hearts' content, but our proclamations will mean nothing—to others or to ourselves—unless we accompany our words with deeds that match. The sermons that we live are far more compelling than the ones we preach.

Like it or not, your life is an accurate reflection of your creed. If this fact gives you some cause for concern, don't bother talking about the changes that you intend to make—make them. And then, when your good deeds speak for themselves—as they most certainly will—don't interrupt.

—.—.—.—.—.—.—

Do nothing that you would not like to be doing when Jesus comes. Go no place where you would not like to be found when He returns.

Corrie ten Boom

ACCEPTANCE FOR TODAY

To You, O my Strength, I will sing praises; for God is my defense, my God of mercy.

Psalm 59:17 NKJV

Manmade plans are fallible; God's plans are not. Yet whenever life takes an unexpected turn, we are tempted to fall into the spiritual traps of worry, self-pity, or bitterness. God intends that we do otherwise.

The old saying is familiar: "Forgive and forget." But when we have been hurt badly, forgiveness is often difficult and forgetting is downright impossible. Since we can't forget yesterday's troubles, we should learn from them. Yesterday has much to teach us about tomorrow. We may learn from the past, but we should never live in the past. God has given each of us a glorious day: this one. And it's up to each of us to use this day as faithful stewards, not as embittered historians.

So if you're trying to forget the past, don't waste your time. Instead, try a different approach: learn to accept the past and live in the present. Then, you can focus your thoughts and your energies, not on the struggles of yesterday, but instead on the profound opportunities that God has placed before you today.

STUDYING GOD'S WORD

Like newborn infants, desire the unadulterated spiritual milk, so that you may grow by it in your salvation.

1 Peter 2:2 Holman CSB

God's Word is unlike any other book. The words of Matthew 4:4 remind us that, "Man shall not live by bread alone but by every word that proceedeth out of the mouth of God" (KJV). As believers, we are instructed to study the Bible and meditate upon its meaning for our lives, yet far too many Bibles are laid aside by well-intentioned believers who would like to study the Bible if they could "just find the time."

Warren Wiersbe observed, "When the child of God looks into the Word of God, he sees the Son of God. And, he is transformed by the Spirit of God to share in the glory of God." God's Holy Word is, indeed, a transforming, life-changing, one-of-a-kind treasure. And it's up to you—and only you—to use it that way.

—.—.—.—.—.—.—

There is no way to draw closer to God unless you are in the Word of God every day. It's your compass. Your guide. You can't get where you need to go without it.

Stormie Omartian

AMAZING GRACE

Saving is all [God's] idea, and all his work. All we do is trust him enough to let him do it. It's God's idea from start to finish! We don't play the major role. If we did, we'd probably go around bragging that we'd done the whole thing! No, we neither make nor save ourselves. God does both the making and the saving.

Ephesians 2:8-9 MSG

Here's the great news: God's grace is not earned . . . and thank goodness it's not! If God's grace were some sort of reward for good behavior, none of us could earn enough brownie points to win the big prize. But it doesn't work that way. Grace is a free offer from God. By accepting that offer, we transform our lives today and forever.

God's grace is not just any old gift; it's the ultimate gift, and we owe Him our eternal gratitude. Our Heavenly Father is waiting patiently for each of us to accept His Son and receive His grace. Let us accept that gift today so that we might enjoy God's presence now and throughout all eternity.

—.—.—.—.—.—.—.—

Yes, God's grace is always sufficient, and His arms are always open to give it. But, will our arms be open to receive it?

Beth Moore

GOD'S GOLDEN RULE

Here is a simple, rule-of-thumb for behavior: Ask yourself what you want people to do for you, then grab the initiative and do it for them. Add up God's Law and Prophets and this is what you get.

Matthew 7:12 MSG

The words of Matthew 7:12 remind us that, as believers in Christ, we are commanded to treat others as we wish to be treated. This commandment is, indeed, the Golden Rule for Christians of every generation. When we weave the thread of kindness into the very fabric of our lives, we give glory to the One who gave His life for ours.

Because we are imperfect human beings, we are, on occasion, selfish, thoughtless, or cruel. But God commands us to behave otherwise. He teaches us to rise above our own imperfections and to treat others with unselfishness and love. When we observe God's Golden Rule, we help build His kingdom here on earth. And, when we share the love of Christ, we share a priceless gift; may we share it today and every day that we live.

—·—·—·—·—·—·—·—

People and labels don't go together. It's much nicer just to push aside the politically correct protocol, snip off the label, and look at each other as . . . people.

Joni Eareckson Tada

TRUST IN A LOVING FATHER

If God is for us, who can be against us?

Romans 8:31 NIV

What do you expect from the day ahead? Are you expecting God to do wonderful things, or are you living beneath a cloud of apprehension and doubt? The familiar words of Psalm 118:24 remind us of a profound yet simple truth: "This is the day which the Lord hath made; we will rejoice and be glad in it" (KJV).

For Christian believers, every day begins and ends with God's Son and God's promises. When we accept Christ into our hearts, God promises us the opportunity for earthly peace and spiritual abundance. But more importantly, God promises us the priceless gift of eternal life.

As we face the inevitable challenges of life-here-on-earth, we must arm ourselves with the promises of God's Holy Word. When we do, we can expect the best, not only for the day ahead, but also for all eternity.

—.—.—.—.—.—.—

How changed our lives would be if we could only fly through the days on wings of surrender and trust!

Hannah Whitall Smith

THE RIGHT KIND OF WISDOM

Only the Lord gives wisdom; he gives knowledge and understanding.

Proverbs 2:6 NCV

The great English preacher, Charles Haddon Spurgeon, once wrote, "Wisdom is the right use of knowledge. To know is not to be wise. Many men know a great deal, and are all the greater fools for it. But to know how to use knowledge is to have wisdom." Spurgeon was, indeed, a very wise man.

To become wise, we must seek God's wisdom and live according to His Word. And, we must not only learn the lessons of the Christian life, we must live by them.

Do you seek to live a life of righteousness and wisdom? If so, you must study the ultimate source of wisdom: the Word of God. You must seek out worthy mentors and listen carefully to their advice. You must associate, day in and day out, with godly men and women. And, you must act in accordance with your beliefs. When you do these things, you will become wise . . . and you will be a blessing to your friends, to your family, and to the world.

—.—.—.—.—.—.—

A big difference exists between a head full of knowledge and the words of God literally abiding in us.

Beth Moore

PATIENCE AND TRUST

Trust in him at all times, O people; pour out your hearts to him, for God is our refuge.

Psalm 62:8 NIV

When times are tough, we want solutions to our problems, and we want them right now! But sometimes, life's greatest challenges defy easy solutions, so we must be patient.

Psalm 37:7 commands us to "Rest in the Lord, and wait patiently for Him" (NKJV). But for most of us, waiting quietly for God is difficult. Why? Because we are imperfect beings who seek solutions to our problems today, if not sooner. We seek to manage our lives according to our own timetables, not God's. To do so is a mistake. Instead of impatiently tapping our fingers, we should fold our fingers and pray. When we do, our Heavenly Father will reward us in His own miraculous way and in His own perfect time.

—.—.—.—.—.—.—

Wait on the Lord, wait patiently, and thou shalt in Him be blest; after the storm, a holy calm, and after thy labor rest.

Fanny Crosby

HIS PROMISES NEVER FAIL

Patient endurance is what you need now, so you will continue to do God's will. Then you will receive all that he has promised.

Hebrews 10:36 NLT

God has made quite a few promises to you, and He intends to keep every single one of them. You will find these promises in a book like no other: the Holy Bible. The Bible is your roadmap for life here on earth and for life eternal—as a believer, you are called upon to trust its promises, to follow its commandments, and to share its Good News.

God has made promises to all of humanity and to you. God's promises never fail and they never grow old. You must trust those promises and share them with your family, with your friends, and with the world . . . starting now . . . and ending never.

—.—.—.—.—.—.—

We have ample evidence that the Lord is able to guide. The promises cover every imaginable situation. All we need to do is to take the hand he stretches out.

Elisabeth Elliot

THE JOY OF SERVING GOD

Enjoy serving the Lord, and he will give you what you want.

Psalm 37:4 NCV

Are you excited about serving God? You should be. As a believer living in today's challenging world, you have countless opportunities to honor your Father in heaven by serving Him.

Far too many Christians seem bored with their faith and stressed by their service. Don't allow yourself to become one of them! Serve God with thanksgiving in your heart and praise on your lips. Make your service to Him a time of celebration and thanksgiving. Worship your Creator by working for Him, joyfully, faithfully, and often.

—.—.—.—.—.—.—.—

God wants us to serve Him with a willing spirit, one that would choose no other way.

Beth Moore

FAITH-FILLED CHRISTIAN

*Cast your burden on the Lord, and He will support you;
He will never allow the righteous to be shaken.*

Psalm 55:22 Holman CSB

Pessimism and Christianity don't mix. Why? Because Christians have every reason to be optimistic about life here on earth and life eternal. As C. H. Spurgeon observed, "Our hope in Christ for the future is the mainstream of our joy." But sometimes, we fall prey to worry, frustration, anxiety, or sheer exhaustion, and our hearts become heavy. What's needed is plenty of rest, a large dose of perspective, and God's healing touch, but not necessarily in that order.

Today, make this promise to yourself and keep it: vow to be a hope-filled Christian. Think optimistically about your life, your future, and your family. Trust your hopes, not your fears. Take time to celebrate God's glorious creation. And then, when you've filled your heart with hope and gladness, share your optimism with others. They'll be better for it, and so will you. But not necessarily in that order.

—·—·—·—·—·—·—

Don't miss the beautiful colors of the rainbow while you're looking for the pot of gold at the end of it!

Barbara Johnson

UNRELIABLE THINKING

Do not worry about anything, but pray and ask God for everything you need, always giving thanks.

Philippians 4:6 NCV

Charles Swindoll advises, "When you're on the verge of throwing a pity party thanks to your despairing thoughts, go back to the Word of God." How true. Self-pity is not only an unproductive way to think, it is also an affront to your Father in heaven. God's Word promises that His children can receive abundance, peace, love, and eternal life. These gifts are not earned; they are an outpouring from God, a manifestation of His grace.

With these rich blessings, how can we, as believers, feel sorry for ourselves? Self-pity and peace cannot coexist in the same mind. Bitterness and joy cannot coexist in the same heart. Thanksgiving and despair are mutually exclusive.

So, if your unreliable thoughts are allowing pain and worry to dominate your life, you must train yourself to think less about your troubles and more about God's blessings. When you stop to think about it, hasn't He given you enough blessings to occupy your thoughts all day, every day, from now on? Of course He has! So focus your mind on Him, and let your worries fend for themselves.

ACTIONS SPEAK LOUDER

In every way be an example of doing good deeds.
When you teach, do it with honesty and seriousness.

Titus 2:7 NCV

Our words speak, but our actions speak much more loudly. And whether we like it or not, all of us are role models. Our friends and family members observe our actions; as followers of Christ, we are obliged to act accordingly.

Corrie ten Boom advised, "Don't worry about what you do not understand. Worry about what you do understand in the Bible but do not live by." And that's sound advice because our families and friends are always watching . . . and so, for that matter, is God.

—.—.—.—.—.—.—

Living life with a consistent spiritual walk deeply influences those we love most.

Vonette Bright

LIVING WITH THE LIVING WORD

Those who listen to instruction will prosper; those who trust the Lord will be happy.

Proverbs 16:20 NLT

Are you sincerely seeking to discover God's will and follow it? If so, study His Word and obey His commandments. The words of Matthew 4:4 remind us that, "Man shall not live by bread alone, but by every word that proceeds from the mouth of God" (NKJV). As believers, we must study the Bible and meditate upon its meaning for our lives. Otherwise, we deprive ourselves of a priceless gift from our Creator.

Jonathan Edwards advised, "Be assiduous in reading the Holy Scriptures. This is the fountain whence all knowledge in divinity must be derived. Therefore let not this treasure lie by you neglected." God's Holy Word is, indeed, a priceless, one-of-a-kind treasure, and a passing acquaintance with the Good Book is insufficient for Christians who seek to obey God's Word and to understand His will. After all, man does not live by bread alone . . .

—·—·—·—·—·—·—

God's Word is a light not only to our path but also to our thinking. Place it in your heart today, and you will never walk in darkness.

Joni Eareckson Tada

FINDING THE NEW AND BETTER WAY

When we were baptized, we were buried with Christ and shared his death. So, just as Christ was raised from the dead by the wonderful power of the Father, we also can live a new life.

Romans 6:4 NCV

For faithful Christians, every day begins and ends with God and with His only begotten Son. Christ came to this earth to give us abundant life and eternal salvation. Our task is to accept Christ's grace with joy in our hearts as we receive the "new life" that can be ours through Him.

Believers who fashion their days around Jesus are transformed: They see the world differently; they act differently, and they feel differently about themselves and their neighbors.

Thoughtful believers face the inevitable challenges and disappointments of each day armed with the joy of Christ and the promise of salvation. So whatever this day holds for you, begin it and end it with God as your partner and Christ as your Savior. And throughout the day, give thanks to the One who created you and saved you. God's love for you is infinite. Accept it joyously and be thankful.

THE POWER OF HOPE

I wait quietly before God, for my hope is in him.

Psalm 62:5 NLT

The self-fulfilling prophecy is alive, well, and living at your house. If you trust God and have faith for the future, your optimistic beliefs will give you direction and motivation. That's one reason that you should never lose hope, but certainly not the only reason. The primary reason that you, as a believer, should never lose hope, is because of God's unfailing promises.

Make no mistake about it: thoughts are powerful things. Your thoughts have the power to lift you up or to hold you down. When you acquire the habit of hopeful thinking, you will have acquired a powerful tool for improving your life. So if you find yourself falling into the spiritual traps of worry and discouragement, seek the healing touch of Jesus and the encouraging words of fellow Christians. And if you fall into the terrible habit of negative thinking, think again. After all, God's Word teaches us that Christ can overcome every difficulty (John 16:33). And when God makes a promise, He keeps it.

—.—.—.—.—.—.—

God's Word never said we were not to grieve our losses. It says we are not to grieve as those who have no hope (1 Thessalonians 4:13). Big Difference.

Beth Moore

LEARNING HOW TO FORGIVE

Above all, keep your love for one another at full strength, since love covers a multitude of sins.

1 Peter 4:8 Holman CSB

Genuine love is an exercise in forgiveness. If we wish to build lasting relationships, we must learn how to forgive. Why? Because our loved ones are imperfect (and so, for that matter, are we).

How often must we forgive our family and friends? More times than we can count. Why? Because that's what God wants us to do.

Perhaps granting forgiveness is hard for you. If so, you are not alone. Genuine, lasting forgiveness is often difficult to achieve—difficult but not impossible. Thankfully, with God's help, all things are possible, and that includes forgiveness. But, even though God is willing to help, He expects you to do some of the work. And make no mistake: forgiveness is work, which is okay with God. He knows that the payoffs are worth the effort.

—·—·—·—·—·—·—

Love is not soft as water is; it is solid as a rock on which the waves of hatred beat in vain.

Corrie ten Boom

OBEDIENCE AND SERVICE

Whoever serves me must follow me. Then my servant will be with me everywhere I am. My Father will honor anyone who serves me.

John 12:26 NCV

God's laws are eternal and unchanging: obedience leads to abundance and joy; disobedience leads to disaster. God has given us a guidebook for righteous living called the Holy Bible. If we trust God's Word and live by it, we are blessed.

Life is a series of decisions and choices. Each day, we make countless decisions that can bring us closer to God . . . or not. When we live according to God's commandments, we earn for ourselves the abundance and peace that He intends for our lives.

Do you seek God's peace and His blessings? Then obey Him. When you're faced with a difficult choice or a powerful temptation, seek God's counsel and trust the counsel He gives. Invite God into your heart and live according to His commandments. When you do, you will be blessed today, tomorrow, and forever.

—·—·—·—·—·—

Peter said, "No, Lord!" But he had to learn that one cannot say "No" while saying "Lord" and that one cannot say "Lord" while saying "No."

Corrie ten Boom

THE POWER OF CHRISTIAN FELLOWSHIP

Behold, how good and how pleasant it is for brethren to dwell together in unity!

Psalm 133:1 NKJV

Fellowship with other believers should be an integral part of your everyday life. Your association with fellow Christians should be uplifting, enlightening, encouraging, and consistent.

Are you an active member of your own fellowship? Are you a builder of bridges inside the four walls of your church and outside it? Do you contribute to God's glory by contributing your time and your talents to a close-knit band of believers? Hopefully so. The fellowship of believers is intended to be a powerful tool for spreading God's Good News and uplifting His children. And God intends for you to be a fully contributing member of that fellowship. Your intentions should be the same.

—.—.—.—.—.—.—.—

In God's economy you will be hard-pressed to find many examples of successful "Lone Rangers."

Luci Swindoll

PRACTICAL CHRISTIANITY

My counsel for you is simple and straightforward: Just go ahead with what you've been given. You received Christ Jesus, the Master; now live him. You're deeply rooted in him. You're well constructed upon him. You know your way around the faith. Now do what you've been taught. School's out; quit studying the subject and start living it! And let your living spill over into thanksgiving.

Colossians 2:6-7 MSG

As Christians, we must do our best to ensure that our actions are accurate reflections of our beliefs. Our theology must be demonstrated, not only by our words but, more importantly, by our actions. In short, we should be practical believers, quick to act whenever we see an opportunity to serve God.

Are you the kind of practical Christian who is willing to dig in and do what needs to be done when it needs to be done? If so, congratulations: God acknowledges your service and blesses it. But if you find yourself more interested in the fine points of theology than in the needs of your neighbors, it's time to rearrange your priorities. God needs believers who are willing to roll up their sleeves and go to work for Him. Count yourself among that number. Theology is a good thing unless it interferes with God's work. And it's up to you to make certain that your theology doesn't.

OUR INTENTIONS ARE IMPORTANT TO GOD

We justify our actions by appearances; God examines our motives.

Proverbs 21:2 MSG

The world sees you as you appear to be; God sees you as you really are. He sees your heart, and He understands your intentions. The opinions of others should be relatively unimportant to you; however, God's view of you—His understanding of your actions, your thoughts, and your motivations—should be vitally important.

Few things in life are more futile than "keeping up appearances" for the sake of neighbors. What is important, of course, is pleasing your Father in heaven. You please Him when your intentions are pure and your actions are just.

—.—.—.—.—.—.—

Outside appearances, things like the clothes you wear or the car you drive, are important to other people but totally unimportant to God. Trust God.

Marie T. Freeman

COURAGE FOR TODAY . . . AND FOREVER

Don't be afraid, because I am your God. I will make you strong and will help you; I will support you with my right hand that saves you.

Isaiah 41:10 NCV

A terrible storm rose quickly on the Sea of Galilee, and the disciples were afraid. Although they had witnessed many miracles, the disciples feared for their lives, so they turned to Jesus, and He calmed the waters and the wind.

Sometimes, we, like Jesus' disciples, feel threatened by the storms of life. When we are fearful, we, too, should turn to Him for comfort and for courage.

The next time you find yourself facing a fear-provoking situation, remember that the One who calmed the wind and the waves is also your personal Savior. Then ask yourself which is stronger: your faith or your fear? The answer should be obvious. So, when the storm clouds form overhead and you find yourself being tossed on the stormy seas of life, remember this: Wherever you are, God is there, too. And, because He cares for you, you are protected.

STRENGTH FOR TOUGH TIMES

If you do nothing in a difficult time, your strength is limited.

Proverbs 24:10 Holman CSB

From time to time, all of us face adversity, hardship, disappointment, and loss. Old Man Trouble pays periodic visits to each of us; none of us are exempt. When we are troubled, God stands ready and willing to protect us. Our responsibility, of course, is to ask Him for protection. When we call upon Him in heartfelt prayer, He will answer—in His own time and in accordance with His own perfect plan.

Our world continues to change, but God's love remains constant. And, He remains ready to comfort us and strengthen us whenever we turn to Him. Psalm 145 promises, "The Lord is near to all who call on him, to all who call on him in truth. He fulfills the desires of those who fear him; he hears their cry and saves them" (vv. 18-20 NIV).

Life is often challenging, but as Christians, we must not be afraid. God loves us, and He will protect us. In times of hardship, He will comfort us; in times of sorrow, He will dry our tears. When we are troubled, weak, or sorrowful, God is always with us. We must build our lives on the rock that cannot be shaken . . . we must trust in God. Always.

EXPECTING GREAT THINGS

When a believing person prays, great things happen.
James 5:16 NCV

James 5:16 makes a promise that God intends to keep: when you pray earnestly, fervently, and often, great things will happen. Too many people, however, are too timid or too pessimistic to ask God to do big things. Don't count yourself among their number.

God can and will do great things through you if you have the courage to ask Him and the determination to keep asking Him. Honor God by making big requests. But don't expect Him to do all the work. When you do your part, He will do His part. And when He does, expect a miracle . . . a big miracle.

—.— **A TIP** —.—

There will be no power in our lives apart from prayer.

WASTED WORDS

A useless person causes trouble, and a gossip ruins friendships.

Proverbs 16:28 NCV

Face it: gossip is bad—and the Bible clearly tells us that gossip is wrong.

When we say things that we don't want other people to know we said, we're being somewhat dishonest, but if the things we say aren't true, we're being very dishonest. Either way, we have done something that we may regret later, especially when the other person finds out.

So do yourself a big favor: don't gossip. It's a waste of words, and it's the wrong thing to do. You'll feel better about yourself if you don't gossip (and other people will feel better about you, too). So don't do it!

—.—.—.—.—.—.—

To belittle is to be little.

Anonymous

PLANNING AND DILIGENCE

The plans of hard-working people earn a profit, but those who act too quickly become poor.

Proverbs 21:5 NCV

Are you willing to plan for the future—and are you willing to work diligently to accomplish the plans that you've made? The Book of Proverbs teaches that the plans of hardworking people (like you) are rewarded.

If you desire to reap a bountiful harvest from life, you must plan for the future while entrusting the final outcome to God. Then, you must do your part to make the future better (by working dutifully), while acknowledging the sovereignty of God's hands over all affairs, including your own.

Are you in a hurry for success to arrive at your doorstep? Don't be. Instead, work carefully, plan thoughtfully, and wait patiently. Remember that you're not the only one working on your behalf: God, too, is at work. And with Him as your partner, your ultimate success is guaranteed.

—.—.—.—.—.—.—.—

Winners see an answer for every problem; losers see a problem in every answer.

Barbara Johnson

ROOM TO GROW

So let us stop going over the basics of Christianity again and again. Let us go on instead and become mature in our understanding.

Hebrews 6:1 NLT

Are you a fully-grown girl? Physically: maybe so. But spiritually? No way! And thank goodness that you're not! Even if you're a very mature person—even if you're a righteous, spiritual, godly woman—you've still got lots of room to grow.

When we cease to grow, either emotionally or spiritually, we do ourselves and our families a profound disservice. But, if we study God's Word, if we obey His commandments, and if we live in the center of His will, we will not be "stagnant" believers; we will, instead, be growing Christians . . . and that's exactly what God wants for our lives. Come to think of it, that's exactly what you should want, too.

—.—.—.—.—.—

God uses our most stumbling, faltering faith-steps as the open door to His doing for us "more than we ask or think."

Catherine Marshall

PLANTING THE SEEDS OF FAITH

Without wavering, let us hold tightly to the hope we say we have, for God can be trusted to keep his promise.

Hebrews 10:23 NLT

Life, like a garden, is a leap of faith. We plant our seeds in God's good earth, and we expect Him to bring forth a plentiful harvest. And so it is when we plant the seeds of faith in our hearts: When we trust God completely, He brings forth a bountiful harvest in our lives, a harvest of abundance, joy, and peace.

Jesus Christ is the ultimate Savior of humanity and the personal Savior of those who believe in Him. As His servants, we must place Him at the very center of our lives, not on the periphery. When we form a personal bond with our Savior, the seeds of our faith will multiply and flourish not only for today, but also for eternity.

—·—·—·—·—·—·—

Faith brings us on highways that make our reasoning dizzy.

Corrie ten Boom

SHINING LIKE STARS

The wise people will shine like the brightness of the sky. Those who teach others to live right will shine like stars forever and ever.

Daniel 12:3 NCV

Our world needs Christian leaders who "will shine like stars forever and ever." Our world needs leaders who willingly honor God with their words and their deeds—with the emphasis on deeds.

If you want to be a godly leader, then you must begin by being a worthy example to your family, to your friends, to your church, and to your community. After all, your words of instruction will never ring true unless you yourself are willing to follow them.

Are you the kind of leader whom you would want to follow? If so, congratulations. But if the answer to that question is no, then it's time to improve your leadership skills, beginning with the words that you speak and the example that you set. And the greatest of these, not surprisingly, is example.

—.—.—.—.—.—.—

We will see more and more that we are chosen not because of our ability but because of the Lord's power, which will be demonstrated in our not being able.

Corrie ten Boom

THE HAND THAT HEALS

I have heard your prayer; I have seen your tears. Look, I will heal you.

2 Kings 20:5 Holman CSB

Are you concerned about your spiritual, physical, or emotional health? And would you like to improve these three areas of your life? If so, there is a timeless source of comfort and assurance that is as near as your bookshelf. That source is the Holy Bible.

God's Word has much to say about every aspect of your life, including your health. And, when you face concerns of any sort—including health-related challenges—God is with you. So trust your medical doctor to do his or her part, but place your ultimate trust in your benevolent Heavenly Father.

Talk to God about your health, seek His guidance, and ask Him for the things you need. When you do, He will hear your prayers, and that's a very good thing because His healing touch, like His love, endures forever.

—.—.—.—.—.—.—.—

Jesus Christ is the One by Whom, for Whom, through Whom everything was made. Therefore, He knows what's wrong in your life and how to fix it.

Anne Graham Lotz

CONCERNING THE STUFF

Prosperity is as short-lived as a wildflower, so don't ever count on it.

James 1:10 MSG

Are you someone who's overly concerned with the stuff that money can buy? Hopefully not. On the grand stage of a well-lived life, material possessions should play a rather small role. Of course, we all need the basic necessities of life, but once we meet those needs for ourselves and for our families, the piling up of possessions creates more problems than it solves. Our real riches, of course, are not of this world. We are never really rich until we are rich in spirit.

Our society is in love with money and the things that money can buy. God is not. God cares about people, not possessions, and so must we. We must, to the best of our abilities, love our neighbors as ourselves, and we must, to the best of our abilities, resist the mighty temptation to place possessions ahead of people.

Money, in and of itself, is not evil; worshipping it is. So today, as you prioritize matters of importance in your life, remember that God is almighty, the dollar is not.

—.—.—.—.—.—.—

As faithful stewards of what we have, ought we not to give earnest thought to our staggering surplus?

Elisabeth Elliot

WORKING WITH HEART AND SOUL

He was diligent in every deed that he began in the service of God's temple, in the law and in the commandment, in order to seek his God, and he prospered.

2 Chronicles 31:21 Holman CSB

How does God intend for us to work? Does He intend for us to work diligently or does He, instead, reward mediocrity? The answer is obvious. God has created a world in which hard work is rewarded and sloppy work is not. Yet sometimes, we may seek ease over excellence, or we may be tempted to take shortcuts when God intends that we walk the straight and narrow path.

Today, heed God's Word by doing good work. Wherever you find yourself, whatever your job description, do your work, and do it with all your heart. When you do, you will most certainly win the recognition of your peers. But more importantly, God will bless your efforts and use you in ways that only He can understand. So do your work with focus and dedication. And leave the rest up to God.

—·—·—·—·—·—·—

You can't climb the ladder of life with your hands in your pockets.

Barbara Johnson

THE POWER OF POSITIVE FRIENDSHIPS

Light shines on those who do right; joy belongs to those who are honest. Rejoice in the Lord, you who do right. Praise his holy name.

Psalm 97:11-12 NCV

Some friendships help us honor God; these friendships should be nurtured. Other friendships place us in situations where we are tempted to dishonor God by disobeying His commandments; friendships that dishonor God have the potential to do us great harm.

Because we tend to become like our friends, we must choose our friends carefully. Because our friends influence us in ways that are both subtle and powerful, we must ensure that our friendships are pleasing to God. When we spend our days in the presence of godly believers, we are blessed, not only by those friends, but also by our Creator.

Do you seek to live a life that is pleasing to God? If so, you should build friendships that are pleasing to Him. When you do, your Heavenly Father will bless you and your friends with gifts that are simply too numerous to count.

WHO RULES?

Do not have other gods besides Me.

Exodus 20:3 Holman CSB

Okay girlfriend, here's a question: Who rules your heart? Is it God, or is it something else? Have you given Christ your heart, your soul, your talents, your time, and your testimony? Or are you giving Him little more than a few hours each Sunday morning?

In the book of Exodus, God warns that we should place no gods before Him. Yet all too often, we place our Lord in second, third, or fourth place as we worship the gods of pride, greed, power, or personal gratification. When we unwittingly place possessions or relationships above our love for the Creator, we must seek His forgiveness and repent from our disobedience.

Does God rule your heart? Make certain that the honest answer to this question is a resounding yes. In the life of every righteous believer, God comes first. And that's precisely the place that He deserves in your heart.

—.—.—.—.—.—.—.—

God prepared a plan for your life alone—and neither man nor the devil can destroy that plan.

Kay Arthur

FACING OUR RESPONSIBILITIES

We want each of you to go on with the same hard work all your lives so you will surely get what you hope for. We do not want you to become lazy. Be like those who through faith and patience will receive what God has promised.

Hebrews 6:11–12 NCV

Nobody needs to tell you the obvious: You have lots of responsibilities—obligations to yourself, to your family, to your community, to your school, and to your God. And which of these duties should take priority? The answer can be found in Matthew 6:33: "But seek first the kingdom of God and His righteousness, and all these things will be provided for you" (Holman CSB).

When you "seek first the kingdom of God," all your other obligations have a way of falling into place. When you obey God's Word and seek His will, your many responsibilities don't seem quite so burdensome. When you honor God with your time, your talents, and your prayers, you'll be much more likely to count your blessings instead of your troubles.

So do yourself and your loved ones a favor: take all your duties seriously, especially your duties to God. When you do, you'll discover that pleasing your Father in heaven isn't just the right thing to do; it's also the best way to live.

THANKING GOD FOR HIS GIFTS

Thanks be to God for his indescribable gift!

2 Corinthians 9:15 NIV

How do we thank God for the gifts He has given us? By using those gifts, that's how!

God has given you talents and opportunities that are uniquely yours. Are you willing to use your gifts in the way that God intends? And are you willing to summon the discipline that is required to develop your talents and to hone your skills? That's precisely what God wants you to do, and that's precisely what you should desire for yourself.

As you seek to expand your talents, you will undoubtedly encounter stumbling blocks along the way, such as the fear of rejection or the fear of failure. When you do, don't stumble! Just continue to refine your skills, and offer your services to God. And when the time is right, He will use you—but it's up to you to be thoroughly prepared when He does.

—.—.—.—.—.—.—

What we are is God's gift to us. What we become is our gift to God.

Anonymous

NEVER GIVE UP

Even though good people may be bothered by trouble seven times, they are never defeated.

Proverbs 24:16 NCV

Do you sincerely want to live a life that is pleasing to God? If so, you must remember that life is not a sprint, it's a marathon that calls for preparation, determination, and lots of perseverance.

Are you one of those people who doesn't give up easily, or are you quick to bail out when the going gets tough? If you've developed the unfortunate habit of giving up at the first sign of trouble, it's probably time for you to have a heart-to-heart talk with the person you see every time you look in the mirror.

Jesus finished what He began, and so should you. Despite His suffering and despite the shame of the cross, Jesus was steadfast in His faithfulness to God. You, too, must remain faithful, especially when times are tough.

Do you want to build a closer relationship with God? Then don't give up. And if you're facing a difficult situation, remember this: whatever your problem, God can handle it. Your job is to keep persevering until He does.

THE CHEERFUL GIVER

God loves the person who gives cheerfully.

2 Corinthians 9:7 NLT

Are you a cheerful giver? If you intend to obey God's commandments, you must be. When you give, God looks not only at the quality of your gift, but also at the condition of your heart. If you give generously, joyfully, and without complaint, you obey God's Word. But, if you make your gifts grudgingly, or if the motivation for your gift is selfish, you disobey your Creator, even if you have tithed in accordance with Biblical principles.

Today, take God's commandments to heart and make this pledge: Be a cheerful, generous, courageous giver. The world needs your help, and you need the spiritual rewards that will be yours when you give faithfully, prayerfully, and cheerfully.

—.—.—.—.—.—.—

When somebody needs a helping hand, he doesn't need it tomorrow or the next day. He needs it now, and that's exactly when you should offer to help. Good deeds, if they are really good, happen sooner rather than later.

Marie T. Freeman

THE WISDOM OF MODERATION

Watch out! Don't let me find you living in careless ease and drunkenness, and filled with the worries of this life. Don't let that day catch you unaware.

Luke 21:34 NLT

Moderation and wisdom are traveling companions. If we are wise, we must learn to temper our appetites, our desires, and our impulses. When we do, we are blessed, in part, because God has created a world in which temperance is rewarded and intemperance is inevitably punished.

Would you like to improve your life? Then harness your appetites and restrain your impulses. Moderation is difficult, of course; it is especially difficult in a prosperous society such as ours. But the rewards of moderation are numerous and long-lasting. Claim those rewards today.

No one can force you to moderate your appetites. The decision to live temperately (and wisely) is yours and yours alone. And so are the consequences.

—.—.—.—.—.—.—

To many, total abstinence is easier than perfect moderation.

St. Augustine

LIVING IN THE SPIRIT OF TRUTH

But when the Spirit of truth comes, he will lead you into all truth.

John 16:13 NCV

God is vitally concerned with truth. His Word teaches the truth; His Spirit reveals the truth; His Son leads us to the truth. When we open our hearts to God, and when we allow His Son to rule over our thoughts and our lives, God reveals Himself, and we come to understand the truth about ourselves and the Truth about God's gift of grace.

The familiar words of John 8:32 remind us that "you shall know the truth, and the truth shall make you free" (NKJV). May we, as believers, seek God's truth and live by it, this day and forever.

—.—.—.—.—.—.—.—

Those who walk in truth walk in liberty.

Beth Moore

THE WISDOM OF THANKSGIVING

It is good to give thanks to the Lord, to sing praises to the Most High. It is good to proclaim your unfailing love in the morning, your faithfulness in the evening.

Psalm 92:1-2 NLT

God's Word makes it clear: a wise heart is a thankful heart. Period. We are to worship God, in part, by the genuine gratitude we feel in our hearts for the marvelous blessings that our Creator has bestowed upon us. Yet even the most saintly among us must endure periods of bitterness, fear, doubt, and regret. Why? Because we are imperfect human beings who are incapable of perfect gratitude. Still, even on life's darker days, we must seek to cleanse our hearts of negative emotions and fill them, instead, with praise, with love, with hope, and with thanksgiving. To do otherwise is to be unfair to ourselves, to our loved ones, and to our God.

—.—.—.—.—.—.—

Thanksgiving or complaining—these words express two contrastive attitudes of the souls of God's children in regard to His dealings with them. The soul that gives thanks can find comfort in everything; the soul that complains can find comfort in nothing.

Hannah Whitall Smith

LEARNING LIFE'S LESSONS . . . THE EASY WAY

Whoever is stubborn after being corrected many times will suddenly be hurt beyond cure.

Proverbs 29:1 NCV

When it comes to learning life's lessons, we can either do things the easy way or the hard way. The easy way can be summed up as follows: when God teaches us a lesson, we learn it . . . the first time! Unfortunately, too many of us learn much more slowly than that.

When we resist God's instruction, He continues to teach, whether we like it or not. Our challenge, then, is to discern God's lessons from the experiences of everyday life. Hopefully, we learn those lessons sooner rather than later because the sooner we do, the sooner He can move on to the next lesson and the next and the next . . .

—.—.—.—.—.—.—

The almighty Father will use life's reverses to move you forward.

Barbara Johnson

THE POSITIVE PATH

But the path of the just is like the shining sun, that shines ever brighter unto the perfect day. The way of the wicked is like darkness; they do not know what makes them stumble.

Proverbs 4:18-19 NKJV

When Jesus addressed His disciples, He warned that each one must, "take up his cross and follow me." The disciples must have known exactly what the Master meant. In Jesus' day, prisoners were forced to carry their own crosses to the location where they would be put to death. Thus, Christ's message was clear: in order to follow Him, Christ's disciples must deny themselves and, instead, trust Him completely. Nothing has changed since then.

If we are to be dutiful disciples of the One from Galilee, we must trust Him and we must follow Him. Jesus never comes "next." He is always first. He shows us the path of life.

Do you want to be a genuine disciple of Jesus? Then pick up His cross today and follow in His footsteps. When you do, you can walk with confidence: He will never lead you astray.

—·—·—·—·—·—

Righteousness comes only from God.

Kay Arthur

CELEBRATING LIFE

Rejoice in the Lord, you righteous ones; praise from the upright is beautiful.

Psalm 33:1 Holman CSB

What is the best day to celebrate life? This one! Today and every day should be a time for celebration as we consider the Good News of God's gift: salvation through Jesus Christ.

What do you expect from the day ahead? Are you expecting God to do wonderful things, or are you living beneath a cloud of worry and doubt?

The familiar words of Psalm 118:24 remind us of a profound yet simple truth: "This is the day which the Lord has made." Our duty, as believers, is to rejoice in God's marvelous creation. For Christians, every day begins and ends with God and His Son. Christ came to this earth to give us abundant life and eternal salvation. We give thanks to our Maker when we treasure each day. So with no further ado, let the celebration begin!

—·—·—·—·—·—·—

Fear and doubt are conquered by a faith that rejoices. And faith can rejoice because the promises of God are as certain as God Himself.

Kay Arthur

COMMENDING OURSELVES TO OTHERS

Therefore, since we have this ministry, as we have received mercy, we do not give up. Instead, we have renounced shameful secret things, not walking in deceit or distorting God's message, but in God's sight we commend ourselves to every person's conscience by an open display of the truth.

2 Corinthians 4:1-2 Holman CSB

God has given us a guidebook for righteous living called the Holy Bible. It contains thorough instructions which, if followed, lead to fulfillment, righteousness and salvation. But, if we choose to ignore God's commandments, the results are as predictable as they are tragic.

A righteous life has many components: faith, honesty, generosity, love, kindness, humility, gratitude, and worship, to name but a few. If we seek to follow the steps of our Savior, Jesus Christ, we must seek to live according to His commandments. In short, we must, to the best of our abilities, live according to the principles contained in God's Holy Word.

So today and every day of your life, study God's Word and live by it. Make your life a shining example for those who have not yet found Christ. Embrace righteousness.

And for further instructions, read the manual.

RETURNING GOD'S LOVE . . . BY SHARING IT

Dear friends, if God loved us in this way, we also must love one another.

1 John 4:11 Holman CSB

God loves you. How will you respond to His love? The Bible clearly defines what your response should be: "You shall love the Lord your God with all your heart, with all your soul, and with all your strength" (Deuteronomy 6:5 NKJV). But you must not stop there. You must also love your neighbor as yourself. Jesus teaches that "On these two commandments hang all the Law and the Prophets" (Matthew 22:40).

Today, as you meet the demands of everyday living, will you pause long enough to return God's love? And then will you share it? Prayerfully, you will. When you embrace God's love, you are forever changed. When you embrace God's love, you feel differently about yourself, your family, your friends, and your world. When you embrace God's love, you have enough love to keep and enough love to share: enough love for a day, enough love for a lifetime, enough love for all eternity.

—·—·—·—·—·—·—

He loved us not because we're lovable, but because He is love.

C. S. Lewis

BEYOND SELF-DECEPTION

If we claim that we're free of sin, we're only fooling ourselves. A claim like that is errant nonsense. On the other hand, if we admit our sins—make a clean breast of them—he won't let us down; he'll be true to himself. He'll forgive our sins and purge us of all wrongdoing.

1 John 1:8-9 MSG

If we ignore our sins or deny them altogether, we allow those sins to flourish. And, if we allow bad behaviors to become bad habits, we invite hardships into our own lives and into the lives of our loved ones.

This world is filled to the brim with distractions and temptations—if we allow ourselves to be sidetracked by the worldliness that surrounds us, we suffer. But God has other intentions . . . and His plans for our lives do not include sin or denial.

If we allow ourselves to encounter God's presence, He will lead us away from temptation, away from confusion, and away from the self-deception. God is the champion of truth and the enemy of denial. May we see ourselves through His eyes and conduct ourselves accordingly.

—.—.—.—.—.—.—

We cannot out-sin God's ability to forgive us.

Beth Moore

COURAGE IS CONTAGIOUS

I will lift up my eyes to the hills—From whence comes my help? My help comes from the Lord, Who made heaven and earth.

Psalm 121:1-2 NKJV

The more we trust God, the more courageously we live. And the more we trust God, the more we can encourage others.

Courage is contagious, and courage inspired by a steadfast trust in a loving Heavenly Father is highly contagious. So today, as you interact with friends, family members, or coworkers, share your courage, your hopes, your dreams, and your enthusiasm. Your positive outlook will be almost as big a blessing to them as it is to you.

—.—.—.—.—.—.—.—

What is courage? It is the ability to be strong in trust, in conviction, in obedience. To be courageous is to step out in faith—to trust and obey, no matter what.

Kay Arthur

WHAT CAN I LEARN TODAY?

It takes knowledge to fill a home with rare and beautiful treasures.

Proverbs 24:4 NCV

If we are to grow as Christians, we need both knowledge and wisdom. Knowledge is found in textbooks. Wisdom, on the other hand, is found in God's Holy Word and in the carefully-chosen words of loving parents, family members, and friends. Knowledge is an important building block in a well-lived life, and it pays rich dividends both personally and professionally. But, wisdom is even more important because it refashions not only the mind, but also the heart.

—·—·—·—·—·—·—

A big difference exists between a head full of knowledge and the words of God literally abiding in us.

Beth Moore

PATIENCE WITH OTHERS AND ONE'S SELF

God has chosen you and made you his holy people.
He loves you. So always do these things: Show mercy to
others, be kind, humble, gentle, and patient.

Colossians 3:12 NCV

The dictionary defines the word *patience* as "the ability to be calm, tolerant, and understanding." If that describes you, you can skip the rest of this page. But, if you're like most of us, you'd better keep reading.

For most of us, patience is a hard thing to master. Why? Because we have lots of things we want, and we want them NOW (if not sooner). But the Bible tells us that we must learn to wait patiently for the things that God has in store for us.

The next time you find your patience tested to the limit, remember that the world unfolds according to God's timetable, not yours. Sometimes, you must wait patiently, and that's as it should be. After all, think how patient God has been with you!

—.—.—.—.—.—.—

The times we find ourselves having to wait on others may be the perfect opportunities to train ourselves to wait on the Lord.

Joni Eareckson Tada

BEYOND OUR FEARS

He replied, "You of little faith, why are you so afraid?"
Then he got up and rebuked the winds and the waves,
and it was completely calm.

Matthew 8:26 NIV

A frightening storm rose quickly on the Sea of Galilee, and the disciples were afraid. Because of their limited faith, they feared for their lives. When they turned to Jesus, He calmed the waters and He rebuked His disciples for their lack of faith in Him.

On occasion, we, like the disciples, are frightened by the inevitable storms of life. Why are we afraid? Because we, like the disciples, possess imperfect faith.

When we genuinely accept God's promises as absolute truth, when we trust Him with life-here-on-earth and life eternal, we have little to fear. Faith in God is the antidote to worry. Faith in God is the foundation of courage and the source of power. Today, let us trust God more completely and, by doing so, move beyond our fears to a place of abundance, assurance, and peace.

—.—.—.—.—.—.—

Only believe, don't fear. Our Master, Jesus, always watches over us, and no matter what the persecution, Jesus will surely overcome it.

Lottie Moon

ABUNDANCE IN THE YEAR AHEAD

My purpose is to give life in all its fullness.

John 10:10 HSCB

Have you made the choice to rejoice? Hopefully so. After all, if you're a believer, you have plenty of reasons to be joyful. Yet sometimes, amid the inevitable hustle and bustle of life, you may lose sight of your blessings as you wrestle with the challenges of everyday life.

Christ made it clear to His followers: He intended that His joy would become their joy. And it still holds true today: Christ intends that His believers share His love with His joy in their hearts.

What does life have in store for you? A world full of possibilities (of course it's up to you to seize them) and God's promise of abundance (of course it's up to you to accept it). So, as you embark upon the next phase of your journey, remember to celebrate the life that God has given you. Your Creator has blessed you beyond measure. Honor Him with your prayers, your words, your deeds, and your joy.

—.—.—.—.—.—.—

Jesus wants Life for us, Life with a capital L.

John Eldredge

GOLDEN RULE

*Here is a simple, rule-of-thumb for behavior: Ask
yourself what you want people to do for you, then grab
the initiative and do it for them. Add up God's Law and
Prophets and this is what you get.*

Matthew 7:12 MSG

Would you like to make the world a better place?
If so, you can start by being a girl who practices the
Golden Rule.

Some rules are easier to understand than they are to
live by, and the Golden Rule certainly fits that description.
Jesus told us that we should treat other people in the same
way that we would want to be treated. But sometimes,
especially when we're tired, upset, jealous, or insecure,
that rule is very hard to follow.

Jesus wants us to treat other people with respect,
kindness, courtesy, and love. When we do, we make our
families and friends happy . . . and we make our Father
in heaven very proud.

So if you're wondering how to make the world a
better place, here's a great place to start: let the Golden
Rule be your rule, too. And if you want to know how to
treat other people, ask the girl you see every time you
look into the mirror. The answer you receive from her will
tell you exactly what to do.

PRAYING FOR PURPOSE

One day Jesus told his disciples a story to illustrate their need for constant prayer and to show them that they must never give up.

Luke 18:1 NLT

Are you faced with a difficult choice or an important decision? Then pray about it. If you talk to God sincerely and often, He won't lead you astray. Instead, God will guide you and help you make more intelligent choices . . . if you take the time to talk with Him.

If you have questions about whether you should do something or not, pray about it. If there is something you're worried about, ask God to comfort you. If you're having trouble with your relationships, ask God to help you sort things out. As you pray more, you'll discover that God is always near and that He's always ready to hear from you. So don't worry about things; pray about them. God is waiting . . . and listening!

—.—.—.—.—.—.—

Through the death and broken body of Jesus Christ on the Cross, you and I have been given access to the presence of God when we approach Him by faith in prayer.

Anne Graham Lotz

HOW MUCH DOES GOD DESERVE?

Freely you have received, freely give.

Matthew 10:8 NIV

What does God deserve from you? Will you give Him the firstfruits of your harvest? Will you honor Him with the best you have to offer? Will you praise the Creator not only with your words but also with your deeds?

Every day is a fresh opportunity to honor God with your prayers, with your praise, with your deeds, and with your testimony. Your Heavenly Father deserves no less.

Does the level of your stewardship honor the One who has given you everything? If so, God will bless you because of your obedience. And if your stewardship has been somehow deficient, the best day to begin serving Him more faithfully is today.

—.—.—.—.—.—.—

We can't do everything, but can we do anything more valuable than invest ourselves in another?

Elisabeth Elliot

IN SEARCH OF PEACE

Peace I leave with you. My peace I give to you. I do not give to you as the world gives. Your heart must not be troubled or fearful.

John 14:27 Holman CSB

The beautiful words of John 14:27 give us hope: "Peace I leave with you, my peace I give unto you . . . ." Jesus offers us peace, not as the world gives, but as He alone gives.

When we accept the peace of Jesus Christ into our hearts, our lives are transformed. And then, because we possess the gift of peace, we can share that gift with fellow Christians, family members, friends, and associates. If, on the other hand, we choose to ignore the gift of peace—for whatever reason—we simply cannot share what we do not possess.

Today, as a gift to yourself, to your family, and to your friends, claim the inner peace that is your spiritual birthright: the peace of Jesus Christ. It is offered freely; it has been paid for in full; it is yours for the asking. So ask. And then share.

—.—.—.—.—.—.—

God is in control of history; it's His story. Doesn't that give you a great peace—especially when world events seems so tumultuous and insane?

Kay Arthur

MOUNTAIN-MOVING FAITH

I tell you the truth, if you have faith as small as a mustard seed, you can say to this mountain, "Move from here to there" and it will move. Nothing will be impossible for you.

Matthew 17:20 NIV

Have you ever felt your faith in God slipping away? If so, you are not alone. Every life—including yours—is a series of successes and failures, celebrations and disappointments, joys and sorrows. But even when we feel very distant from God, God is never distant from us.

Jesus taught His disciples that if they had faith, they could move mountains. You can too. When you place your faith, your trust, indeed your life in the hands of Christ Jesus, you'll be amazed at the marvelous things He can do with you and through you. So strengthen your faith through praise, through worship, through Bible study, and through prayer. And trust God's plans. With Him, all things are possible, and He stands ready to open a world of possibilities to you if you have faith.

—.—.—.—.—.—.—.—

Faith in faith is pointless. Faith in a living, active God moves mountains.

Beth Moore

PRAISE FOR THE FATHER

From the rising of the sun to its setting, the name of the Lord is to be praised.

Psalm 113:3 NASB

Okay, from the looks of things, you're an extremely busy girl. And perhaps, because of your demanding schedule, you've neglected to pay sufficient attention to a particularly important part of your life: the spiritual part. If so, today is the day to change, and one way to make that change is simply to spend a little more time talking with God.

God is trying to get His message through to you. Are you listening?

Perhaps, on occasion, you may find yourself overwhelmed by the press of everyday life. Perhaps you may forget to slow yourself down long enough to talk with God. Instead of turning your thoughts and prayers to Him, you may rely upon our own resources. Instead of asking God for guidance, you may depend only upon your own limited wisdom. A far better course of action is this: simply stop what you're doing long enough to open your heart to God; then listen carefully for His directions.

In all things great and small, seek God's wisdom and His grace. He hears your prayers, and He will answer. All you must do is ask.

IMITATING OUR SAVIOR

If you love me, you will obey what I command.

John 14:15 NIV

Imitating Christ is impossible, but attempting to imitate Him is both possible and advisable. By attempting to imitate Jesus, we seek, to the best of our abilities, to walk in His footsteps. To the extent we succeed in following Him, we receive the spiritual abundance that is the rightful possession of those who love Christ and keep His commandments.

Do you seek God's blessings for the day ahead? Then, to the best of your abilities, imitate His Son. You will fall short, of course. But if your heart is right and your intentions are pure, God will bless your efforts, your day, and your life.

—.— A TIP —.—

The whole idea of belonging to Christ is to look less and less like we used to and more and more like Him.

THE OPTIMISTIC CHRISTIAN

Make me hear joy and gladness.

Psalm 51:8 NKJV

As you take the next step in your life's journey, you should do so with feelings of hope and anticipation. After all, as a Christian, you have every reason to be optimistic about life. As John Calvin observed, "There is not one blade of grass, there is no color in this world that is not intended to make us rejoice." But, sometimes, rejoicing may be the last thing on your mind. Sometimes, you may fall prey to worry, frustration, anxiety, or sheer exhaustion. What's needed is plenty of rest, a large dose of perspective, and God's healing touch, but not necessarily in that order.

A. W. Tozer writes, "Attitude is all-important. Let the soul take a quiet attitude of faith and love toward God, and from there on, the responsibility is God's. He will make good on His commitments." These words remind us that even when the challenges of the day seem daunting, God remains steadfast. And, so must we.

—.—.—.—.—.—.—

Stop thinking wishfully and start living hopefully.

Emilie Barnes

FINDING TIME FOR GOD

I am always praising you; all day long I honor you.

Psalm 71:8 NCV

Each new day is a gift from God, and if we are wise, we will spend a few quiet moments each morning thanking the Giver. Daily life is a tapestry of habits, and no habit is more important to our spiritual health than the discipline of daily prayer and devotion to the Creator. When we begin each day with heads bowed and hearts lifted, we remind ourselves of God's love, His protection, and His commandments. And if we are wise, we take time throughout the day to align our priorities with the teachings and commandments that God has given us through His Holy Word.

Are you thankful for God's blessings? Then give Him a gift that demonstrates your gratitude: the gift of time.

—.—.—.—.—.—.—.—

Are you weak? Weary? Confused? Troubled? Pressured? How is your relationship with God? Is it held in its place of priority? I believe the greater the pressure, the greater your need for time alone with Him.

Kay Arthur

A FRESH START

I will give you a new heart and put a new spirit in you . . . .

Ezekiel 36:26 NIV

Each new day offers countless opportunities to serve God, to seek His will, and to obey His teachings. But each day also offers countless opportunities to stray from God's commandments and to wander far from His path.

Sometimes, we wander aimlessly in a wilderness of our own making, but God has better plans for us. And, whenever we ask Him to renew our strength and guide our steps, He does so.

Consider this day a new beginning. Consider it a fresh start, a renewed opportunity to serve your Creator with willing hands and a loving heart. Ask God to renew your sense of purpose as He guides your steps. Today is a glorious opportunity to serve God. Seize that opportunity while you can; tomorrow may indeed be too late.

—.—.—.—.—.—.—

Repentance removes old sins and wrong attitudes, and it opens the way for the Holy Spirit to restore our spiritual health.

Shirley Dobson

KEEPING LIFE IN PERSPECTIVE

All I'm doing right now, friends, is showing how these things pertain to Apollos and me so that you will learn restraint and not rush into making judgments without knowing all the facts. It is important to look at things from God's point of view. I would rather not see you inflating or deflating reputations based on mere hearsay.

1 Corinthians 4:6 MSG

If a temporary loss of perspective has left you worried, exhausted, or both, it's time to readjust your thought patterns. Negative thoughts are habit-forming; thankfully, so are positive ones. With practice, you can form the habit of focusing on God's priorities and your own possibilities. When you do, you'll soon discover that you will spend less time fretting about your challenges and more time praising God for His gifts.

When you call upon the Lord and prayerfully seek His will, He will give you wisdom and perspective. When you make God's priorities your priorities, He will direct your steps and calm your fears. So today and every day hereafter, pray for a sense of balance and perspective. And remember: no problems are too big for God—and that includes yours.

COURAGE FOR EVERYDAY LIVING

God doesn't want us to be shy with his gifts, but bold and loving and sensible.

2 Timothy 1:7 MSG

Life-here-on-earth can be difficult and discouraging at times. During our darkest moments, God offers us strength and courage if we turn our hearts and our prayers to Him.

As believing Christians, we have every reason to live courageously. After all, the ultimate battle has already been fought and won on the cross at Calvary. But sometimes, because we are imperfect human beings who possess imperfect faith, we fall prey to fear and doubt. The answer to our fears, of course, is God.

The next time you find your courage tested to the limit, remember that God is as near as your next breath. He is your shield and your strength; He is your protector and your deliverer. Call upon Him in your hour of need and then be comforted. Whatever your challenge, whatever your trouble, God can handle it . . . and will!

—.—.—.—.—.—.—

If a person fears God, he or she has no reason to fear anything else. On the other hand, if a person does not fear God, then fear becomes a way of life.

Beth Moore

FINDING GOD'S PURPOSE IN EVERYDAY LIFE

Do not be afraid or discouraged. For the Lord your God is with you wherever you go.

Joshua 1:9 NLT

Each morning, as the sun rises in the east, you welcome a new day, one that is filled to the brim with opportunities, with possibilities, and with God. As you contemplate God's blessings in your own life, you should prayerfully seek His guidance for the day ahead.

Discovering God's unfolding purpose for your life is a daily journey, a journey guided by the teachings of God's Holy Word. As you reflect upon God's promises and upon the meaning that those promises hold for you, ask God to lead you throughout the coming day. Let your Heavenly Father direct your steps; concentrate on what God wants you to do now, and leave the distant future in hands that are far more capable than your own: His hands.

—.—.—.—.—.—.—

We are most vulnerable to the piercing winds of doubt when we distance ourselves from the mission and fellowship to which Christ has called us.

Joni Eareckson Tada

THE BREAD OF LIFE

*Then Jesus said, "I am the bread that gives life.
Whoever comes to me will never be hungry, and
whoever believes in me will never be thirsty."*

John 6:35 NCV

He was the Son of God, but He wore a crown of
thorns. He was the Savior of mankind, yet He was put to
death on a roughhewn cross made of wood. He offered
His healing touch to an unsaved world, and yet the same
hands that had healed the sick and raised the dead were
pierced with nails.

Jesus Christ, the Son of God, was born into humble
circumstances. He walked this earth, not as a ruler of
men, but as the Savior of mankind. His crucifixion, a
torturous punishment that was intended to end His life
and His reign, instead became the pivotal event in the
history of all humanity.

Jesus is the bread of life. Accept His grace. Share His
love. And follow His footsteps.

—.—.—.—.—.—.—

Jesus was the Savior who would deliver them not only
from the bondage of sin but also from meaningless
wandering through life.

Anne Graham Lotz

THE POWER OF PRAYER

Therefore I say to you, whatever things you ask when you pray, believe that you receive them, and you will have them.

Mark 11:24 NKJV

In case you've been wondering, wonder no more—God does answer your prayers. What God does not do is this: He does not always answer your prayers as soon as you might like, and He does not always answer your prayers by saying "Yes."

God isn't an order-taker, and He's not some sort of cosmic vending machine. Sometimes—even when we want something very badly—our loving Heavenly Father responds to our requests by saying "No," and we must accept His answer, even if we don't understand it.

God answers prayers not only according to our wishes but also according to His master plan. We cannot know that plan, but we can know the Planner . . . and we must trust His wisdom, His righteousness, and His love.

Of this you can be sure: God is listening, and He wants to hear from you now.

—.—.—.—.—.—.—

Whatever may be our circumstances in life, may each one of us really believe that by way of the Throne we have unlimited power.

Annie Armstrong

WHEN IN DOUBT . . .

Don't depend on your own wisdom. Respect the Lord and refuse to do wrong.

Proverbs 3:7 NCV

If you're like most young women, you're busy . . . very busy. And sometimes, because so much is expected of you, you may lose perspective. Your life may seem to be spinning out of control, and the pressures of everyday living seem overwhelming. What's needed is a fresh perspective, a restored sense of balance . . . and God's wisdom.

Would you really like to become wise? If so, learning about wisdom isn't enough. You must also behave wisely. Wisdom is as wisdom does. Wisdom is determined, not by words, but by deeds.

Do you wish to walk among the wise? If so, you must walk wisely. There is simply no other way.

—.—.—.—.—.—.—

We must lay our questions, frustrations, anxieties, and impotence at the feet of God and wait for His answer. And then receiving it, we must live by faith.

Kay Arthur

PUTTING OFF TILL TOMORROW

If you make a promise to God, don't be slow to keep it. God is not happy with fools, so give God what you promised.

Ecclesiastes 5:4 NCV

The habit of procrastination takes a two-fold toll on its victims. First, important work goes unfinished; second, valuable energy is wasted in the process of putting off the things that remain undone. Procrastination results from an individual's short-sighted attempt to postpone temporary discomfort. What results is a senseless cycle of 1. delay, followed by 2. worry, followed by 3. a panicky and often futile attempt to "catch up." Procrastination is, at its core, a struggle against oneself; the only antidote is action.

Once you acquire the habit of doing what needs to be done when it needs to be done, you will avoid untold trouble, worry, and stress. So learn to defeat procrastination by paying less attention to your fears and more attention to your responsibilities. God has created a world that punishes procrastinators and rewards men and women who "do it now." In other words, life doesn't procrastinate. Neither should you.

DISCOVERING GOD'S PURPOSE IN TIMES OF ADVERSITY

In this world you will have trouble. But take heart! I have overcome the world.

John 16:33 NIV

The Bible promises this: tough times are temporary but God's love is not—God's love lasts forever. So what does that mean to you? Just this: From time to time, everybody faces tough times, and so will you. And when tough times arrive, God will always stand ready to protect you and heal you.

Psalm 147 promises, "He heals the brokenhearted" (v. 3, NIV), but Psalm 147 doesn't say that He heals them instantly. Usually, it takes time (and maybe even a little help from you) for God to fix things. So if you're facing tough times, face them with God by your side. If you find yourself in any kind of trouble, pray about it and ask God for help. And be patient. God will work things out, just as He has promised, but He will do it in His own way and in His own time.

—.—.—.—.—.—.—

When we face an impossible situation, all self-reliance and self-confidence must melt away; we must be totally dependent on Him for the resources.

Anne Graham Lotz

PRAISING GOD'S GLORIOUS CREATION

The heavens declare the glory of God, and the sky proclaims the work of His hands.

Psalm 19:1 Holman CSB

Each morning, the sun rises upon a glorious world that is a physical manifestation of God's infinite power and His infinite love. And yet we're sometimes too busy to notice.

We live in a society filled with more distractions than we can possibly count and more obligations than we can possibly meet. Is it any wonder, then, that we often overlook God's handiwork as we rush from place to place, giving scarcely a single thought to the beauty that surrounds us?

Today, take time to really observe the world around you. Take time to offer a prayer of thanks for the sky above and the beauty that lies beneath it. And take time to ponder the miracle of God's creation. The time you spend celebrating God's wonderful world is always time well spent.

—.—.—.—.—.—.—

Heaven and earth and all that is in the universe cry out to me from all directions that I, O God, must love You.

St. Augustine

GOD'S TIMETABLE

There is an occasion for everything, and a time for every activity under heaven.

Ecclesiastes 3:1 Holman CSB

Most of us are impatient for God to grant us the desires of our heart. Usually, we know what we want, and we know precisely when we want it: right now, if not sooner. But God may have other plans. And when God's plans differ from our own, we must trust in His infinite wisdom and in His infinite love.

As busy people living in a fast-paced world, many of us find that waiting quietly for God is difficult. Why? Because we are imperfect human beings seeking to live according to our own timetables, not God's. In our better moments, we realize that patience is not only a virtue, but it is also a commandment from the Creator.

God instructs us to be patient in all things. We must be patient with our families, with our friends, and with our acquaintances. We must also be patient with our Heavenly Father as He unfolds His plan for our lives. And that's as it should be. After all, think how patient God has been with us.

—·—·—·—·—·—

God gave everyone patience—wise people use it.

Anonymous

STRENGTH FOR TODAY

The Lord is my strength and my song; He has become my salvation.

Exodus 15:2 Holman CSB

Where do you go to find strength? The gym? The health food store? The espresso bar? There's a better source of strength, of course, and that source is God. He is a never-ending source of strength and courage if you call upon Him.

Have you "tapped in" to the power of God? Have you turned your life and your heart over to Him, or are you muddling along under your own power? The answer to this question will determine the quality of your life here on earth and the destiny of your life throughout all eternity. So start tapping in—and remember that when it comes to strength, God is the Ultimate Source.

—·—·—·—·—·—·—

The amount of power you experience to live a victorious, triumphant Christian life is directly proportional to the freedom you give the Spirit to be Lord of your life!

Anne Graham Lotz

TRUSTING THE FUTURE TO GOD

"I say this because I know what I am planning for you," says the Lord. *"I have good plans for you, not plans to hurt you. I will give you hope and a good future."*

Jeremiah 29:11 NCV

How bright is your future? Well, if you're willing to go over the edge for God, then your future is so bright that you'd better bring shades and sunscreen. But here's another important question: How bright do you believe your future to be? Are you expecting a terrific tomorrow, or are you dreading a terrible one? The answer you give will have a powerful impact on the way tomorrow turns out.

Do you trust in the ultimate goodness of God's plan for your life? Will you face tomorrow's challenges with optimism and hope? You should. After all, God created you for a very important reason: His reason. And you still have important work to do: His work.

Today, as you live in the present and look to the future, remember that God has an amazing plan for you. Act—and believe—accordingly.

—.—.—.—.—.—

Never be afraid to trust an unknown future to a known God.

Corrie ten Boom

THE POWER OF OUR THOUGHTS

Set your minds on what is above, not on what is on the earth.

Colossians 3:2 Holman CSB

Our thoughts have the power to lift us up or drag us down; they have the power to energize us or deplete us, to inspire us to greater accomplishments, or to make those accomplishments impossible.

God intends that you experience joy and abundance, but He will not impose His joy upon you; you must accept it for yourself. It's up to you to celebrate the life that God has given you by focusing your mind upon "whatever is of good repute" (Philippians 4:8). Today, spend more time thinking about God's blessings, and less time fretting about the minor inconveniences of life. Then, take time to thank the Giver of all things good for gifts that are glorious, miraculous, and eternal.

—.—.—.—.—.—.—

The things we think are the things that feed our souls. If we think on pure and lovely things, we shall grow pure and lovely like them; and the converse is equally true.

Hannah Whitall Smith

GOD MAKES ALL THINGS POSSIBLE

You are the God who does wonders; You have declared Your strength among the peoples.

Psalm 77:14 NKJV

Sometimes, because we are imperfect human beings with limited understanding and limited faith, we place limitations on God. But, God's power has no limitations. God will work miracles in our lives if we trust Him with everything we have and everything we are. When we do, we experience the miraculous results of His endless love and His awesome power.

Do you lack the faith that God can work miracles in your own life? If so, it's time to reconsider. Are you filled with doubts? If so, you are attempting to place limitations on a God who has none. Instead, you must trust in God and trust in His power. Then, you must wait patiently . . . because something miraculous is just about to happen.

—.—.—.—.—.—.—

I believe that God is in the miracle business—that his favorite way of working is to pick up where our human abilities and understandings leave off and then do something so wondrous and unexpected that there's no doubt who the God is around here.

Emilie Barnes

A THANKFUL HEART

Enter his gates with thanksgiving; go into his courts with praise. Give thanks to him and bless his name. For the Lord is good. His unfailing love continues forever, and his faithfulness continues to each generation.

Psalm 100:4-5 NLT

If you're like most females on the planet, you're a very busy girl. Your life is probably hectic, demanding, and complicated. When the demands of life leave you rushing from place to place with scarcely a moment to spare, you may fail to pause and thank your Creator for the blessings He has bestowed upon you. Big mistake.

No matter how busy you are, you should never be too busy to thank God for His gifts. Your task, as a follower of the living Christ, is to praise God many times each day. Then, with gratitude in your heart, you can face your daily duties with the perspective and power that only He can provide.

When you slow down and express your gratitude to your Heavenly Father, you enrich your own life and the lives of those around you. That's why thanksgiving should become a habit, a regular part of your daily routine. Yes, God has blessed you beyond measure, and you owe Him everything, including your eternal praise.

THE WISDOM OF SILENCE

My soul, wait silently for God alone, For my expectation is from Him.

Psalm 62:5 NKJV

Are you a girl who takes time each day for silence? And during those precious moments, do you sincerely open your heart to your Creator? If so, you are wise and you are blessed.

The world can be a noisy place, a place filled to the brim with distractions, interruptions, and frustrations. And if you're not careful, the struggles and stresses of everyday living can rob you of the peace that should rightfully be yours because of your personal relationship with Christ. So take time each day to quietly commune with your Savior. When you do, those moments of silence will enable you to participate more fully in the only source of peace that endures: God's peace.

—.—.—.—.—.—.—

When an honest soul can get still before the living Christ, we can still hear Him say simply and clearly, "Love the Lord your God with all your heart and with all your soul and with all your mind . . . and love one another as I have loved you."

Gloria Gaither

ASKING GOD

Your Father knows exactly what you need even before you ask him!

Matthew 6:8 NLT

Sometimes, amid the demands and the frustrations of everyday life, we forget to slow ourselves down long enough to talk with God. Instead of turning our thoughts and prayers to Him, we rely instead upon our own resources. Instead of praying for strength and courage, we seek to manufacture it within ourselves. Instead of asking God for guidance, we depend only upon our own limited wisdom. The results of such behaviors are unfortunate and, on occasion, tragic.

Are you in need? Ask God to sustain you. Are you troubled? Take your worries to Him in prayer. Are you weary? Seek God's strength. In all things great and small, seek God's wisdom and His grace. He hears your prayers, and He will answer. All you must do is ask.

—.—.—.—.—.—.—.—

When will we realize that we're not troubling God with our questions and concerns? His heart is open to hear us—his touch nearer than our next thought—as if no one in the world existed but us. Our very personal God wants to hear from us personally.

Gigi Graham Tchividjian

PUTTING POSSESSIONS IN PROPER PERSPECTIVE

No one can serve two masters. The person will hate one master and love the other, or will follow one master and refuse to follow the other. You cannot serve both God and worldly riches.

Matthew 6:24 NCV

"So much stuff to shop for, and so little time . . ." These words seem to describe the priorities of our 21st-century world. Hopefully, you're not building your life around your next visit to the local mall—but you can be sure that many people are!

Our society is in love with money and the things that money can buy. God is not. God cares about people, not possessions, and so must we. We must, to the best of our abilities, love our neighbors as ourselves, and we must, to the best of our abilities, resist the mighty temptation to place possessions ahead of people.

Money, in and of itself, is not evil; worshipping money is. So today, as you prioritize matters of importance for you and yours, remember that God is almighty, but the dollar is not.

If we worship God, we are blessed. But if we worship "the almighty dollar," we are inevitably punished because of our misplaced priorities—and our punishment inevitably comes sooner rather than later.

RECEIVING GOD IN THE PRESENT TENSE

Love the Lord your God with all your heart and with all your soul and with all your strength.

Deuteronomy 6:5 NIV

God's love for you is deeper and more profound than you can imagine. God's love for you is so great that He sent His only Son to this earth to die for your sins and to offer you the priceless gift of eternal life. Now, you must decide whether or not to accept God's gift. Will you ignore it or embrace it? Will you return it or neglect it? Will you accept Christ's love and build a lifelong relationship with Him, or will you turn away from Him and take a different path?

Your decision to allow Christ to reign over your heart is the pivotal decision of your life. It is a decision that you cannot ignore. It is a decision that is yours and yours alone. Accept God's gift now: allow His Son to preside over your heart, your thoughts, and your life, starting this very instant.

—.—.—.—.—.—.—

Every person who has ever been born has the sovereign right to make this same choice—to receive Jesus Christ by faith as God's revelation of Himself, or to reject Him.

Anne Graham Lotz

A SOCIETY BRIMMING WITH TEMPTATIONS

But remember that the temptations that come into your life are no different from what others experience. And God is faithful. He will keep the temptation from becoming so strong that you can't stand up against it. When you are tempted, he will show you a way out so that you will not give in to it.

1 Corinthians 10:13 NLT

Face it: You live in a temptation-filled world. The devil is working hard at work in your neighborhood, and so are his helpers. Here in the 21st Century, the bad guys are working around the clock to lead you astray. That's why you must remain vigilant.

In a letter to believers, Peter offers a stern warning: "Your adversary, the devil, prowls around like a roaring lion, seeking someone to devour" (I Peter 5:8 NASB). What was true in New Testament times is equally true in our own. Satan tempts his prey and then devours them (and it's up to you—and only you—to make sure that you're not one of the ones being devoured!).

As a believer who seeks a radical relationship with Jesus, you must beware because temptations are everywhere. Satan is determined to win; you must be equally determined that he does not.

THE JOYS OF FELLOWSHIP

Then all the people went away to eat and drink, to send some of their food to others, and to celebrate with great joy. They finally understood what they had been taught.

Nehemiah 8:12 NCV

If you genuinely want to build a closer relationship with God, you need to build closer relationships with godly people. That's why fellowship with like-minded believers should be an integral part of your life. Your association with fellow Christians should be uplifting, enlightening, encouraging, and (above all) consistent.

Are your friends the kind of people who encourage you to seek God's will and to obey God's Word? If so, you've chosen your friends wisely. And that's a good thing because when you choose friends who honor God, you'll find it easier to honor Him, too.

—.—.—.—.—.—.—.—

One of the ways God refills us after failure is through the blessing of Christian fellowship. Just experiencing the joy of simple activities shared with other children of God can have a healing effect on us.

Anne Graham Lotz

OBEDIENCE TO THE FATHER

But prove yourselves doers of the word, and not merely hearers.

James 1:22 NASB

God's commandments are not "suggestions," and they are not "helpful hints." They are, instead, immutable laws which, if followed, lead to repentance, salvation, and abundance. But if you choose to disobey the commandments of your Heavenly Father or the teachings of His Son, you will most surely reap a harvest of regret.

The formula for a successful life is surprisingly straightforward: Study God's Word and obey it. Does this sound too simple? Perhaps it is simple, but it is also the only way to reap the marvelous riches that God has in store for you.

—.—.—.—.—.—.—

Experience has taught me that the Shepherd is far more willing to show His sheep the path than the sheep are to follow. He is endlessly merciful, patient, tender, and loving. If we, His stupid and wayward sheep, really want to be led, we will without fail be led. Of that I am sure.

Elisabeth Elliot

OUR PROBLEMS = GOD'S OPPORTUNITIES

As for God, his way is perfect. All the Lord's promises prove true. He is a shield for all who look to him for protection.

Psalm 18:30 NLT

Here's a riddle: What is it that is too unimportant to pray about yet too big for God to handle? The answer, of course, is: "nothing." Yet sometimes, when the challenges of the day seem overwhelming, we may spend more time worrying about our troubles than praying about them. And, we may spend more time fretting about our problems than solving them. A far better strategy is to pray as if everything depended entirely upon God and to work as if everything depended entirely upon us.

What we see as problems God sees as opportunities. And if we are to trust Him completely, we must acknowledge that even when our own vision is dreadfully impaired, His vision is perfect. Today and every day, let us trust God by courageously confronting the things that we see as problems and He sees as possibilities.

—·—·—·—·—·—·—

What a comfort to know that God is present there in your life, available to meet every situation with you, that you are never left to face any problem alone.

Vonette Bright

GRACE FOR TODAY

My grace is sufficient for you, for my power is made perfect in weakness.

2 Corinthians 12:9 NIV

God's grace is not earned . . . thank goodness! To earn God's love and His gift of eternal life would be far beyond the abilities of even the most righteous man or woman. Thankfully, God's grace is not an earthly reward for righteous behavior; it is a blessed spiritual gift that can be accepted by believers who dedicate themselves to God through Christ. When we accept Christ into our hearts, we are saved by His grace.

As you contemplate the day ahead, praise God for His blessings. He is the Giver of all things good. He is the Comforter, the Protector, the Teacher, and the Savior. Praise Him today and forever.

—.—.—.—.—.—.—

We will never cease to need our Father—His wisdom, direction, help, and support. We will never outgrow Him. We will always need His grace.

Kay Arthur

SCATTERING SEEDS OF KINDNESS

Be devoted to one another in brotherly love. Honor one another above yourselves.

Romans 12:10 NIV

What is a friend? The dictionary defines the word *friend* as "a person who is attached to another by feelings of affection or personal regard." This definition is accurate, as far as it goes, but when we examine the deeper meaning of friendship, so many more descriptors come to mind: trustworthiness, loyalty, helpfulness, kindness, understanding, forgiveness, encouragement, humor, and cheerfulness, to mention but a few.

How wonderful are the joys of friendship! Today, as you consider the many blessings that God has given you, remember to thank Him for the friends He has chosen to place along your path. May you be a blessing to them, and may they richly bless you today, tomorrow, and every day that you live.

—.—.—.—.—.—.—

A person who really cares about his or her neighbor, a person who genuinely loves others, is a person who bears witness to the truth.

Anne Graham Lotz

FOLLOWING IN THE FOOTSTEPS

Whoever serves me must follow me. Then my servant will be with me everywhere I am. My Father will honor anyone who serves me.

John 12:26 NCV

If you genuinely want to make choices that are pleasing to God, you must ask yourself this question: "How does God want me to serve others?"

Whatever your age, wherever you happen to be, you may be certain of this: service to others is an integral part of God's plan for your life.

Every single day of your life, including this one, God will give you opportunities to serve Him by serving other people. Welcome those opportunities with open arms. They are God's gift to you, His way of allowing you to achieve greatness in His kingdom.

—·—·—·—·—·—

So many times we say that we can't serve God because we aren't whatever is needed. We're not talented enough or smart enough or whatever. But if you are in covenant with Jesus Christ, He is responsible for covering your weaknesses, for being your strength. He will give you His abilities for your disabilities!

Kay Arthur

LIVING ABOVE THE DAILY WHINE

Do everything readily and cheerfully—no bickering, no second-guessing allowed! Go out into the world uncorrupted, a breath of fresh air in this squalid and polluted society. Provide people with a glimpse of good living and of the living God. Carry the light-giving Message into the night.

Philippians 2:14-15 MSG

Sometimes, we lose sight of our blessings. Ironically, most of us have more blessings than we can count, but we may still find reasons to complain about the minor frustrations of everyday life. To do so, of course, is not only wrong; it is also the pinnacle of shortsightedness and a serious roadblock on the path to spiritual abundance.

Are you tempted to complain about the inevitable minor frustrations of everyday living? Don't do it! Today and every day, make it a practice to count your blessings, not your hardships. It's the truly decent way to live.

—.—.—.—.—.—.—

Attitude is the mind's paintbrush; it can color any situation.

Barbara Johnson

TRUSTING GOD'S WORD

Jesus answered, "It is written: 'Man does not live by bread alone, but on every word that comes from the mouth of God.'"

Matthew 4:4 NIV

The Bible is unlike any other book. As Christians, we are called upon to share God's Holy Word with a world in desperate need of His healing hand. The Bible is a priceless gift, a tool for Christians to use as they share the Good News of their Savior, Christ Jesus. Too many Christians, however, keep their spiritual tool kits tightly closed and out of sight.

Jonathan Edwards advised, "Be assiduous in reading the Holy Scriptures. This is the fountain whence all knowledge in divinity must be derived. Therefore let not this treasure lie by you neglected." God's Holy Word is, indeed, a priceless, one-of-a-kind treasure. Handle it with care, but more importantly, handle it every day.

—.—.—.—.—.—.—

If we are not continually fed with God's Word, we will starve spiritually.

Stormie Omartian

WHAT KIND OF EXAMPLE?

You should be an example to the believers in speech, in conduct, in love, in faith, in purity.

1 Timothy 4:12 Holman CSB

Whether we like it or not, all of us are examples. The question is not whether we will be examples to our families and friends; the question is simply what kind of examples will we be?

What kind of example are you? Are you the kind of person whose life serves as a powerful example of righteousness? Are you a young woman whose behavior serves as a positive role model for younger folks? Are you the kind of young woman whose actions, day in and day out, are honorable, ethical, and admirable? If so, you are not only blessed by God, but you are also a powerful force for good in a world that desperately needs positive influences such as yours.

D. L. Moody advised, "A man ought to live so that everybody knows he is a Christian, and most of all, his family ought to know." And that's sound advice because our families and friends are watching . . . and so, for that matter, is God.

—·—·—·—·—·—·—

More depends on my walk than my talk.

D. L. Moody

DAY BY DAY WITH GOD

Uphold my steps in Your paths, that my footsteps may not slip.

Psalm 17:5 NKJV

Our world is in a state of constant change. God is not. At times, the world seems to be trembling beneath our feet. But we can be comforted in the knowledge that our Heavenly Father is the rock that cannot be shaken. His Word promises, "I am the Lord, I do not change" (Malachi 3:6 NKJV).

Every day that we live, we mortals encounter a multitude of changes—some good, some not so good. And on occasion, all of us must endure life-changing personal losses that leave us breathless. When we do, our loving Heavenly Father stands ready to protect us, to comfort us, to guide us, and, in time, to heal us.

Are you facing difficult circumstances or unwelcome changes? If so, please remember that God is far bigger than any problem you may face. So, instead of worrying about life's inevitable challenges, put your faith in the Father and His only begotten Son: Jesus Christ is the same yesterday, today, and forever (Hebrews 13:8). And rest assured: It is precisely because your Savior does not change that you can face your challenges with courage for this day and hope for the future.

MORE OPPORTUNITIES THAN WE CAN COUNT

Everything is possible to the one who believes.

Mark 9:23 Holman CSB

Whether you realize it or not, opportunities are whirling around you like stars crossing the night sky: beautiful to observe but too numerous to count. Yet you may be too wrapped up in the daily grind to notice.

Take time to step back from the challenges of everyday living so that you can focus your thoughts on two things: the talents God has given you and the opportunities that He has placed before you. God is leading you in the direction of those opportunities. Your task is to watch carefully, to pray fervently, and to act accordingly.

—.— A TIP —.—

Unbelief keeps us living beneath the possibilities that God dreamed for our lives.

ABOVE AND BEYOND OUR WORRIES

So don't worry about tomorrow, because tomorrow will have its own worries. Each day has enough trouble of its own.

Matthew 6:34 NCV

When we're worried, there are two places we should take our concerns: to the people who love us and to God.

When troubles arise, it helps to talk about them with parents, grandparents, concerned adults, and trusted friends. But we shouldn't stop there: we should also talk to God through our prayers.

If you're worried about something, pray about it. Remember that God is always listening, and He always wants to hear from you.

So when you're upset about something, try this simple plan: talk and pray. Talk openly to the people who love you, and pray to the Heavenly Father who made you. The more you talk and the more you pray, the better you'll feel.

—.—.—.—.—.—.—.—

Worry does not empty tomorrow of its sorrow; it empties today of its strength.

Corrie ten Boom

PRAYER: MORE IS BETTER

Rejoice always, pray without ceasing, in everything give thanks; for this is the will of God in Christ Jesus for you.

1 Thessalonians 5:16-18 NKJV

Is prayer an integral part of your daily life, or is it a hit-or-miss habit? Do you "pray without ceasing," or is your prayer life an afterthought? Do you regularly pray in the solitude of the early morning darkness, or do you bow your head only when others are watching?

The quality of your spiritual life will be in direct proportion to the quality of your prayer life. Prayer changes things, and it changes you. Today, instead of turning things over in your mind, turn them over to God in prayer. Instead of worrying about your next decision, ask God to lead the way. Don't limit your prayers to meals or to bedtime. Pray constantly about things great and small. God is listening, and He wants to hear from you.

—.—.—.—.—.—.—.—

Often I have made a request of God with earnest pleadings even backed up with Scripture, only to have Him say "No" because He had something better in store.

Ruth Bell Graham

WHEN THE PATH IS DARK

Though I sit in darkness, the Lord will be my light.

Micah 7:8 Holman CSB

Doubts come in several shapes and sizes: doubts about God, doubts about the future, and doubts about our own abilities, for starters. But when doubts creep in, as they will from time to time, we need not despair. As Sheila Walsh observed, "To wrestle with God does not mean that we have lost faith, but that we are fighting for it."

God never leaves our side, not for an instant. He is always with us, always willing to calm the storms of life. When we sincerely seek His presence—and when we genuinely seek to establish a deeper, more meaningful relationship with Him—God is prepared to touch our hearts, to calm our fears, to answer our doubts, and to restore our confidence.

—·—·—·—·—·—·—

I was learning something important: we are most vulnerable to the piercing winds of doubt when we distance ourselves from the mission and fellowship to which Christ has called us. Our night of discouragement will seem endless and our task impossible, unless we recognize that He stands in our midst.

Joni Eareckson Tada

TRUSTING YOUR CONSCIENCE

Do not be conquered by evil, but conquer evil with good.

Romans 12:21 Holman CSB

Billy Graham correctly observed, "Most of us follow our conscience as we follow a wheelbarrow. We push it in front of us in the direction we want to go." To do so, of course, is a profound mistake. Yet all of us, on occasion, have failed to listen to the voice that God planted in our hearts, and all of us have suffered the consequences.

God gave you a conscience for a very good reason: to make your path conform to His will. Wise believers make it a practice to listen carefully to that quiet internal voice. Count yourself among that number. When your conscience speaks, listen and learn. In all likelihood, God is trying to get His message through. And in all likelihood, it is a message that you desperately need to hear.

—.—.—.—.—.—.—

To go against one's conscience is neither safe nor right. Here I stand. I cannot do otherwise.

Martin Luther

LIVING AND WORKING PASSIONATELY

In all the work you are doing, work the best you can.
Work as if you were doing it for the Lord, not for people.

Colossians 3:23 NCV

Are you passionate about your life, your loved ones, your work, and your faith? As a believer who has been saved by a risen Christ, you should be.

As a thoughtful Christian, you have every reason to be enthusiastic about life, but sometimes the struggles of everyday living may cause you to feel decidedly unenthusiastic. If you feel that your zest for life is slowly fading away, it's time to slow down, to rest, to count your blessings, and to pray. When you feel worried or weary, you must pray fervently for God to renew your sense of wonderment and excitement.

Life with God is a glorious adventure; revel in it. When you do, God will most certainly smile upon your work and your life.

—.—.—.—.—.—.—

Wouldn't it make astounding difference, not only in the quality of the work we do, but also in the satisfaction, even our joy, if we recognized God's gracious gift in every single task?

Elisabeth Elliot

HOW THEY KNOW THAT WE KNOW

Here's how we can be sure that we know God in the right way: Keep his commandments. If someone claims, "I know him well!" but doesn't keep his commandments, he's obviously a liar. His life doesn't match his words. But the one who keeps God's word is the person in whom we see God's mature love. This is the only way to be sure we're in God. Anyone who claims to be intimate with God ought to live the same kind of life Jesus lived.

1 John 2:3-6 MSG

How do others know that we are followers of Christ? By our words and by our actions. And when it comes to proclaiming our faith, the actions we take are far more important than the proclamations we make.

Is your conduct a worthy example for believers and non-believers alike? Is your behavior a testimony to the spiritual abundance that is available to those who allow Christ to reign over their hearts? If so, you are wise: congratulations. But if you're like most of us, then you know that some important aspect of your life could stand improvement. If so, today is the perfect day to make yourself a living, breathing example of the wonderful changes that Christ can make in the lives of those who choose to walk with Him.

THE COMPANY YOU KEEP

Do not be misled: "Bad company corrupts good character."

1 Corinthians 15:33 NIV

Our world is filled with pressures: some good, some bad. The pressures that we feel to follow God's will and to behave responsibly are positive pressures. God places them on our hearts, and He intends that we act accordingly. But we also face different pressures, ones that are definitely not from God. When we feel pressured to do things—or even to think thoughts—that lead us away from God, we must beware.

Society seeks to mold us into the cookie-cutter images that are the product of the modern media. God seeks to mold us into new beings, new creations through Christ, beings that are most certainly not conformed to this world. If we are to please God, we must resist the pressures that society seeks to impose upon us, and we must conform ourselves, instead, to His will, to His path, and to His Son.

—.—.—.—.—.—.—

We, as God's people, are not only to stay far away from sin and sinners who would entice us, but we are to be so like our God that we mourn over sin.

Kay Arthur

MARY, MARTHA, AND THE MASTER

You will teach me how to live a holy life. Being with you will fill me with joy; at your right hand I will find pleasure forever.

Psalm 16:11 NCV

Martha and Mary were sisters who both loved Jesus, but they showed their love in different ways. Mary sat at the Master's feet, taking in every word. Martha, meanwhile, busied herself with preparations for the meal to come. When Martha asked Jesus if He was concerned about Mary's failure to help, Jesus replied, "Mary has chosen the better thing, and it will never be taken away from her" (Luke 10:42 NCV). The implication is clear: as believers, we must spend time with Jesus before we spend time for him. But, once we have placed Christ where He belongs—at the center of our hearts—we must go about the business of serving the One who has saved us.

How can we serve Christ? By sharing His message, His mercy, and His love with those who cross our paths. Everywhere we look, it seems, the needs are great and so are the temptations. Still, our challenge is clear: we must love God, obey His commandments, trust His Son, and serve His children. When we do, we claim spiritual treasures that will endure forever.

BEYOND BITTERNESS

Those who show mercy to others are happy, because God will show mercy to them.

Matthew 5:7 NCV

Are you mired in the quicksand of bitterness or regret? If so, you are not only disobeying God's Word, you are also wasting your time. The world holds few if any rewards for those who remain angrily focused upon the past. Still, the act of forgiveness is difficult.

Being frail, fallible, imperfect human beings, most of us are quick to anger, quick to blame, slow to forgive, and even slower to forget. Yet as Christians, we are commanded to forgive others, just as we, too, have been forgiven.

If there exists even one person—alive or dead— against whom you hold bitter feelings, it's time to forgive. Or, if you are embittered against yourself for some past mistake or shortcoming, it's finally time to forgive yourself and move on. Hatred, bitterness, and regret are not part of God's plan for your life. Forgiveness is.

—.—.—.—.—.—.—

Forgiveness is the key that unlocks the door of resentment and the handcuffs of hate. It is a power that breaks the chains of bitterness and the shackles of selfishness.

Corrie ten Boom

REALLY LIVING MEANS REALLY LOVING

And may the Lord cause you to increase and overflow with love for one another and for everyone, just as we also do for you.

1 Thessalonians 3:12 Holman CSB

Christ's words are clear: we are to love God first, and secondly, we are to love others as we love ourselves (Matthew 22:37-40). These two commands are seldom easy, and because we are imperfect beings, we often fall short. But God's Holy Word commands us to try.

The Christian path is an exercise in love and forgiveness. If we are to walk in Christ's footsteps, we must forgive those who have done us harm, and we must accept Christ's love by sharing it freely with family, friends, neighbors, and strangers.

—·—·—·—·—·—·—

It is when we come to the Lord in our nothingness, our powerlessness and our helplessness that He then enables us to love in a way which, without Him, would be absolutely impossible.

Elisabeth Elliot

PRAYERFUL PATIENCE

The Lord is good to those whose hope is in him, to the one who seeks him; it is good to wait quietly for the salvation of the Lord.

Lamentations 3:25-26 NIV

We human beings are, by our very nature, impatient. We are impatient with others, impatient with ourselves, and impatient with our Creator. We want things to happen according to our own timetables, but our Heavenly Father may have other plans. That's why we must learn the art of patience.

Psalm 37:7 commands us to "rest in the Lord, and wait patiently for Him" (NKJV). But, for most of us, waiting patiently for Him is difficult. Why? Because we are fallible human beings who seek solutions to our problems today, if not sooner. Still, God instructs us to wait patiently for His plans to unfold, and that's exactly what we should do.

So the next time you find yourself drumming your fingers as you wait for a quick resolution to the challenges of everyday living, take a deep breath and ask God for patience. Be still before your Heavenly Father and trust His timetable: it's the peaceful way to live.

A HUMBLE SPIRIT

*But he who is greatest among you shall be your servant.
And whoever exalts himself will be humbled, and he
who humbles himself will be exalted.*

Matthew 23:11-12 NLT

God's Word clearly instructs us to be humble. And that's good because, as fallible human beings, we have so very much to be humble about! Yet some of us continue to puff ourselves up, seeming to say, "Look at me!" To do so is wrong.

As Christians, we have been refashioned and saved by Jesus Christ, and that salvation came not because of our own good works but because of God's grace. How, then, can we be prideful? The answer, of course, is that, if we are honest with ourselves and with our God, we simply can't be boastful . . . we must, instead, be eternally grateful and exceedingly humble. The good things in our lives, including our loved ones, come from God. He deserves the credit—and we deserve the glorious experience of giving it to Him.

—.—.—.—.—.—.—

If you know who you are in Christ, your personal ego is not an issue.

Beth Moore

ASKING AND ACCEPTING

So I say to you, keep asking, and it will be given to you. Keep searching, and you will find. Keep knocking, and the door will be opened to you.

Luke 11:9 Holman CSB

God gives the gifts; we, as believers, should accept them—but oftentimes, we don't. Why? Because we fail to trust our Heavenly Father completely, and because we are, at times, surprisingly stubborn. Luke 11 teaches us that God does not withhold spiritual gifts from those who ask. Our obligation, quite simply, is to ask for them.

Are you asking God to move mountains in your life, or are you expecting Him to stumble over molehills? Whatever the size of your challenges, God is big enough to handle them. Ask for His help today, with faith and with fervor, and then watch in amazement as your mountains begin to move.

—.—.—.—.—.—.—

When will we realize that we're not troubling God with our questions and concerns? His heart is open to hear us—his touch nearer than our next thought—as if no one in the world existed but us. Our very personal God wants to hear from us personally.

Gigi Graham Tchividjian

QUESTIONS AND ANSWERS

Listen carefully to wisdom; set your mind on understanding.

Proverbs 2:2 NCV

Each day has 1,440 minutes—can you give God at least five minutes each day? And make no mistake about it: the emphasis in the previous sentence should be placed on the words "at least." In truth, you should give God lots more time than a measly five minutes, but hey, it's a start.

Has the busy pace of life robbed you of time with God? If so, it's time to reorder your priorities and your life. Nothing is more important than the time you spend with your Heavenly Father, so slow down and have a word or two with Him. Then, claim the peace and abundance that can be yours when you regularly spend time with your Heavenly Father. His peace is offered freely; it has been paid for in full; it is yours for the asking.

—.—.—.—.—.—.—

If you are struggling to make some difficult decisions right now that aren't specifically addressed in the Bible, don't make a choice based on what's right for someone else. You are the Lord's and He will make sure you do what's right.

Lisa Whelchel

BUILDING CHARACTER, MOMENT BY MOMENT

May integrity and uprightness protect me, because my hope is in you.

Psalm 25:21 NIV

It has been said that character is what we are when nobody is watching. How true. But, as Bill Hybels correctly observed, "Every secret act of character, conviction, and courage has been observed in living color by our omniscient God." And isn't that a sobering thought?

When we do things that we know aren't right, we try to hide our misdeeds from family members and friends. But even then, God is watching.

If you sincerely wish to walk with God, you must seek, to the best of your ability, to follow His commandments. When you do, your character will take care of itself . . . and you won't need to look over your shoulder to see who, besides God, is watching.

—.—.—.—.—.—.—

Sow an act, and you reap a habit. Sow a habit and you reap a character. Sow a character and you reap a destiny.

Anonymous

LOVE GOD AND GET BUSY

So don't get tired of doing what is good. Don't get discouraged and give up, for we will reap a harvest of blessing at the appropriate time.

Galatians 6:9 NLT

The old saying is both familiar and true: actions speak louder than words. And as believers, we must beware: our actions should always give credence to the changes that Christ can make in the lives of those who walk with Him.

God calls upon each of us to act in accordance with His will and with respect for His commandments. If we are to be responsible believers, we must realize that it is never enough simply to hear the instructions of God; we must also live by them. And it is never enough to wait idly by while others do God's work here on earth; we, too, must act. Doing God's work is a responsibility that each of us must bear, and when we do, our loving Heavenly Father rewards our efforts with a bountiful harvest.

—·—·—·—·—·—

God has lots of folks who intend to go to work for him "some day." What He needs is more people who are willing to work for Him this day.

Marie T. Freeman

FINDING THE PURPOSE BENEATH THE PROBLEM

Be joyful because you have hope. Be patient when trouble comes, and pray at all times.

Romans 12:12 NCV

Hidden beneath every problem is the seed of a solution—God's solution. Your challenge, as a faithful believer, is to trust God's providence and seek His solutions. When you do, you will eventually discover that God does nothing without a very good reason: His reason.

Are you willing to faithfully trust God on good days and bad ones? Hopefully so, because an important part of walking with God is finding His purpose in the midst of your problems.

—.—.—.—.—.—.—.—

Looking back, I can see that the most exciting events of my life have all risen out of trouble.

Catherine Marshall

LIVING IN AN ANXIOUS WORLD

Don't fret or worry. Instead of worrying, pray. Let petitions and praises shape your worries into prayers, letting God know your concerns. Before you know it, a sense of God's wholeness, everything coming together for good, will come and settle you down. It's wonderful what happens when Christ displaces worry at the center of your life.

Philippians 4:6-7 MSG

We live in a world that seems to invite panic. Everywhere we turn, or so it seems, we are confronted with disturbing images that seem to cry out. "All is lost." But with God, there is always hope.

God calls us to live above and beyond anxiety. God calls us to live by faith, not by fear. He instructs us to trust Him completely, this day and forever. But sometimes, trusting God is difficult, especially when we become caught up in the incessant demands of an anxious world.

When you feel anxious—and you will—return your thoughts to God's love. Then, take your concerns to Him in prayer and, to the best of your ability, leave them there. Whatever "it" is, God is big enough to handle it. Let Him . . . now!

HOLINESS BEFORE HAPPINESS

Blessed are those who hunger and thirst for righteousness, for they will be filled.

Matthew 5:6 NIV

Because you are an imperfect human being, you are not "perfectly" happy—and that's perfectly okay with God. He is far less concerned with your happiness than He is with your holiness.

God continuously reveals Himself in everyday life, but He does not do so in order to make you contented; He does so in order to lead you to His Son. So don't be overly concerned with your current level of happiness: it will change. Be more concerned with the current state of your relationship with Christ: He does not change. And because your Savior transcends time and space, you can be comforted in the knowledge that in the end, His joy will become your joy . . . for all eternity.

—.—.—.—.—.—.—.—

Holiness isn't in a style of dress. It's not a matter of rules and regulations. It's a way of life that emanates quietness and rest, joy in family, shared pleasures with friends, the help of a neighbor—and the hope of a Savior.

Joni Eareckson Tada

HE IS HERE

Every morning he wakes me. He teaches me to listen like a student. The Lord God helps me learn . . .

Isaiah 50:4-5 NCV

Do you ever wonder if God is really here? If so, you're not the first person to think such thoughts. In fact, some of the biggest heroes in the Bible had their doubts—and so, perhaps, will you. But when questions arise and doubts begin to creep into your mind, remember this: God hasn't gone on vacation; He hasn't left town; and He doesn't have an unlisted number. You can talk with Him any time you feel like it. In fact, He's right here, right now, listening to your thoughts and prayers, watching over your every move.

Sometimes, you will allow yourself to become very busy, and that's when you may be tempted to ignore God. But, when you quiet yourself long enough to acknowledge His presence, God will touch your heart and restore your spirits. By the way, He's ready to talk right now. Are you?

—.—.—.—.—.—.—

God makes prayer as easy as possible for us. He's completely approachable and available, and He'll never mock or upbraid us for bringing our needs before Him.

Shirley Dobson

LIVING ON PURPOSE

God chose you to be his people, so I urge you now to live the life to which God called you.

Ephesians 4:1 NCV

Life is best lived on purpose. And purpose, like everything else in the universe, begins with God. Whether you realize it or not, God has a plan for your life, a divine calling, a direction in which He is leading you. When you welcome God into your heart and establish a genuine relationship with Him, He will begin, in time, to make His purposes known.

Sometimes, God's intentions will be clear to you; other times, God's plan will seem uncertain at best. But even on those difficult days when you are unsure which way to turn, you must never lose sight of these overriding facts: God created you for a reason; He has important work for you to do; and He's waiting patiently for you to do it.

And the next step is up to you.

—.—.—.—.—.—.—

There is something about having endured great loss that brings purity of purpose and strength of character.

Barbara Johnson

HELPING THE HELPLESS

I have shown you in every way, by laboring like this, that you must support the weak. And remember the words of the Lord Jesus, that He said, "It is more blessed to give than to receive."

Acts 20:35 NKJV

God's hand is merciful and loving; God's gifts are beyond description; God's blessings are beyond comprehension; God has been incredibly generous with us, and He rightfully expects us be generous with others.

The thread of generosity is woven into the very fabric of Christ's teachings. As He sent His disciples out to heal the sick and to spread God's message of salvation, Jesus offered this guiding principle: "Freely you have received, freely give" (Matthew 10:8 NKJV). The principle still applies.

If we are to be disciples of Christ, we must give freely of our time, our possessions, and our love—just as God has been generous with us. As believers, we are blessed here on earth, and we are blessed eternally through God's grace. We can never fully repay God for His gifts, but we can share them with others. And we should.

—·—·—·—·—·—

You can't light another's path without casting light on your own.

John Maxwell

NO SHORTCUTS

Take care of your own business, and do your own work as we have already told you. If you do, then people who are not believers will respect you, and you will not have to depend on others for what you need.

1 Thessalonians 4:11-12 NCV

The world often tempts us with instant gratification: get rich—today; lose weight—today; have everything you want—today. Yet life's experiences and God's Word tell us that the best things in life require heaping helpings of both time and work.

It has been said, quite correctly, that there are no shortcuts to any place worth going. For believers, it's important to remember that hard work is not simply a proven way to get ahead; it's also part of God's plan for His children.

So do yourself this favor: don't look for shortcuts . . . because there aren't any.

—.—.—.—.—.—.—

Great relief and satisfaction can come from seeking God's priorities for us in each season, discerning what is "best" in the midst of many noble opportunities, and pouring our most excellent energies into those things.

Beth Moore

FACING OUR FEARS

I, even I, am the Lord, and apart from me there is no Savior.

Isaiah 43:11 NIV

All of us may find our courage tested by the inevitable disappointments and tragedies of life. After all, ours is a world filled with uncertainty, hardship, sickness, and danger. Old Man Trouble, it seems, is never too far from the front door.

When we focus upon our fears and our doubts, we may find many reasons to lie awake at night and fret about the uncertainties of the coming day. A better strategy, of course, is to focus not upon our fears, but instead upon our God.

God is as near as your next breath, and He is in control. He offers salvation to all His children, including you. God is your shield and your strength; you are His forever. So don't focus your thoughts upon the fears of the day. Instead, trust God's plan and His eternal love for you. And remember: God is good, and He always has the last word.

—·—·—·—·—·—·—

Whether our fear is absolutely realistic or out of proportion in our minds, our greatest refuge is Jesus Christ.

Luci Swindoll

THE LIFE OF MODERATION

Do you want to be counted wise, to build a reputation for wisdom? Here's what you do: Live well, live wisely, live humbly. It's the way you live, not the way you talk, that counts.

James 3:13 MSG

When we allow our appetites to run wild, they usually do. When we abandon moderation and focus, instead, on consumption, we forfeit the inner peace that God offers—but does not guarantee—to His children. When we live intemperate lives, we rob ourselves of countless blessings that would have otherwise been ours.

God's instructions are clear: If we seek to live wisely, we must be moderate in our appetites and disciplined in our behavior. To do otherwise is an affront to Him . . . and to ourselves.

—.—.—.—.—.—

Virtue—even attempted virtue—brings light; indulgence brings fog.

C. S. Lewis

WHEN CHANGE IS PAINFUL

We are pressured in every way but not crushed; we are perplexed but not in despair.

2 Corinthians 4:8 Holman CSB

When life unfolds according to our wishes, or when we experience unexpected good fortune, we find it easy to praise God's plan. That's when we greet change with open arms. But sometimes the changes that we must endure are painful. When we struggle through the difficult days of life, as we must from time to time, we may ask ourselves, "Why me?" The answer, of course, is that God knows, but He isn't telling . . . yet.

Have you endured a difficult transition that has left your head spinning or your heart broken? If so, you have a clear choice to make: either you can cry and complain, or you can trust God and get busy fixing what's broken. The former is a formula for disaster; the latter is a formula for a well-lived life.

—.—.—.—.—.—.—

The undeniable gospel is this: a transformed life.

Liz Curtis Higgs

PROSPERITY, PROMISES, AND PEACE

The Lord's blessing brings wealth, and no sorrow comes with it.

Proverbs 10:22 NCV

We live in an era of prosperity, a time when many of us have been richly blessed with an assortment of material possessions that our ancestors could have scarcely imagined. As believers living in these prosperous times, we must be cautious: We must keep prosperity in perspective.

The world stresses the importance of material possessions; God does not. The world offers the promise of happiness through fame and fortune; God offers the promise of peace through His Son.

When in doubt, we must distrust the world and trust God. The world often makes promises that it cannot keep, but when God makes a promise, He keeps it, not just for a day or a year or a lifetime, but for all eternity.

—.—.—.—.—.—.—.—

Our ultimate aim in life is not to be healthy, wealthy, prosperous, or problem free. Our ultimate aim in life is to bring glory to God.

Anne Graham Lotz

NAVIGATING DEAD END STREETS

He gives strength to the weary, and to him who lacks might He increases power.

Isaiah 40:29 NASB

As we travel the roads of life, all of us are confronted with streets that seem to be dead ends. When we do, we may become discouraged. After all, we live in a society where expectations can be high and demands even higher.

If you find yourself enduring difficult circumstances, remember that God remains in His heaven. If you become discouraged with the direction of your day or your life, turn your thoughts and prayers to Him. He is a God of possibility, not negativity. He will guide you through your difficulties and beyond them. And then, with a renewed spirit of optimism and hope, you can thank the Giver of all things good for gifts that are simply too profound to fully understand and for treasures that are too numerous to count.

—.—.—.—.—.—.—.—

We must leave it to God to answer our prayers in His own wisest way. Sometimes, we are so impatient and think that God does not answer. God always answers! He never fails! Be still. Abide in Him.

Mrs. Charles E. Cowman

TIME FOR REST

Are you tired? Worn out? Burned out on religion? Come to me. Get away with me and you'll recover your life. I'll show you how to take a real rest. Walk with me and work with me . . . watch how I do it. Learn the unforced rhythms of grace. I won't lay anything heavy or ill-fitting on you. Keep company with me and you'll learn to live freely and lightly.

Matthew 11:28-30 MSG

Even the most inspired Christians can, from time to time, find themselves "running out of steam." If you currently fit that description, remember that God expects you to do your work, but He also intends for you to rest. When you fail to take time for sufficient rest, you do a disservice to yourself, to your family, and to your friends.

Is your energy on the wane? Is your spiritual tank near empty? Are your emotions frayed? If so, it's time to turn your thoughts and your prayers to God. And when you're finished, it's time to treat yourself to a heaping helping of "R&R" which, in this case, stands for "Rest and Renewal."

—.—.—.—.—.—.—

Life is strenuous. See that your clock does not run down.

Mrs. Charles E. Cowman

A LIFE OF PRAYER

May the words of my mouth and the meditation of my heart be acceptable to You, Lord, my rock and my Redeemer.

Psalm 19:14 Holman CSB

Prayer is a powerful tool for communicating with our Creator; it is an opportunity to commune with the Giver of all things good. Prayer is not a thing to be taken lightly or to be used infrequently. Prayer should never be reserved for mealtimes or for bedtimes; it should be an ever-present focus in our daily lives.

In his first letter to the Thessalonians, Paul wrote, "Rejoice evermore. Pray without ceasing. In every thing give thanks: for this is the will of God in Christ Jesus concerning you" (5:17-18 KJV). Paul's words apply to every Christian of every generation.

Today, instead of turning things over in our minds, let us turn them over to God in prayer. Instead of worrying about our decisions, let's trust God to help us make them. Today, let us pray constantly about things great and small. God is listening, and He wants to hear from us. Now.

—·—·—·—·—·—·—

Life is fragile—handle with prayer.

Anonymous

PUTTING FAITH TO THE TEST

Even though good people may be bothered by trouble seven times, they are never defeated.

Proverbs 24:16 NCV

Life is a tapestry of good days and difficult days, with good days predominating. During the good days, we are tempted to take our blessings for granted (a temptation that we must resist with all our might). But, during life's difficult days, we discover precisely what we're made of. And more importantly, we discover what our faith is made of.

Has your faith been put to the test yet? If so, then you know that with God's help, you can endure life's darker days. But if you have not yet faced the inevitable trials and tragedies of life, don't worry: you will. And when your faith is put to the test, rest assured that God is perfectly willing—and always ready—to give you strength for the struggle.

—.—.—.—.—.—.—.—

Walking in faith brings you to the Word of God. There you will be healed, cleansed, fed, nurtured, equipped, and matured.

Kay Arthur

SHARING THE GOOD NEWS

As you go, preach this message: "The kingdom of heaven is near."

Matthew 10:7 NIV

After His resurrection, Jesus addressed His disciples: *But the eleven disciples proceeded to Galilee, to the mountain which Jesus had designated. When they saw Him, they worshiped Him; but some were doubtful. And Jesus came up and spoke to them, saying, "All authority has been given to Me in heaven and on earth." "Go therefore and make disciples of all the nations, baptizing them in the name of the Father and the Son and the Holy Spirit, teaching them to observe all that I commanded you; and lo, I am with you always, even to the end of the age"* (Matthew 28:16–20 NASB).

Christ's great commission applies to Christians of every generation, including our own. As believers, we are called to share the Good News of Jesus Christ with our families, with our neighbors, and with the world. Jesus commanded His disciples to become fishers of men. We must do likewise, and we must do so today. Tomorrow may indeed be too late.

THE PATH

But grow in the special favor and knowledge of our Lord and Savior Jesus Christ. To him be all glory and honor, both now and forevermore. Amen.

2 Peter 3:18 NLT

When will you be a "fully-grown" Christian woman? Hopefully never—or at least not until you arrive in heaven! As a believer living here on planet earth, you're never "fully grown"; you always have the potential to keep growing.

In those quiet moments when you open your heart to God, the One who made you keeps remaking you. He gives you direction, perspective, wisdom, and courage.

Would you like a time-tested formula for spiritual growth? Here it is: keep studying God's Word, keep obeying His commandments, keep praying (and listening for answers), and keep trying to live in the center of God's will. When you do, you'll never stay stuck for long. You will, instead, be a growing Christian . . . and that's precisely the kind of Christian God wants you to be.

—.—.—.—.—.—.—

Although God most assuredly wills that His children study Scripture thoroughly, scholarship is not His main goal for us. Relationship is.

Beth Moore

THE WAY WE TREAT OUR NEIGHBORS

The whole law is made complete in this one command:
"Love your neighbor as you love yourself."

Galatians 5:14 NCV

How should we treat other people? God's Word is clear: we should treat others in the same way that we wish to be treated. This Golden Rule is easy to understand, but sometimes it can be difficult to live by.

Because we are imperfect human beings, we are, on occasion, selfish, thoughtless, or cruel. But God commands us to behave otherwise. He teaches us to rise above our own imperfections and to treat others with unselfishness and love. When we observe God's Golden Rule, we help build His kingdom here on earth. And, when we share the love of Christ, we share a priceless gift; may we share it today and every day that we live.

—.—.—.—.—.—

The cross that Jesus commands you and me to carry is the cross of submissive obedience to the will of God, even when His will includes suffering and hardship and things we don't want to do.

Anne Graham Lotz

HAPPINESS IS . . .

Happy are the people who live at your Temple . . . .
Happy are those whose strength comes from you.

Psalm 84:4-5 NKJV

Do you seek happiness, abundance, and content-ment? If so, here are some things you should do: Love God and His Son; depend upon God for strength; try, to the best of your abilities, to follow God's will; and strive to obey His Holy Word. When you do these things, you'll discover that happiness goes hand-in-hand with righteousness. The happiest people are not those who rebel against God; the happiest people are those who love God and obey His commandments.

What does life have in store for you? A world full of possibilities (of course it's up to you to seize them), and God's promise of abundance (of course it's up to you to accept it). So, as you embark upon the next phase of your journey, remember to celebrate the life that God has given you. Your Creator has blessed you beyond measure. Honor Him with your prayers, your words, your deeds, and your joy.

—.—.—.—.—.—.—.—

Those who have had to wait and work for happiness seem to enjoy it more, because they never take it for granted.

Barbara Johnson

CHOICES PLEASING TO GOD

I am offering you life or death, blessings or curses. Now, choose life! Then you and your children may live. To choose life is to love the Lord your God, obey him, and stay close to him.

Deuteronomy 30:19-20 NCV

Because we are creatures of free will, we make choices—lots of them. When we make choices that are pleasing to our Heavenly Father, we are blessed. When we make choices that cause us to walk in the footsteps of God's Son, we enjoy the abundance that Christ has promised to those who follow Him. But when we make choices that are displeasing to God, we sow seeds that have the potential to bring forth a bitter harvest.

Today, as you encounter the challenges of everyday living, you will make hundreds of choices. Choose wisely. Make your thoughts and your actions pleasing to God. And remember: every choice that is displeasing to Him is the wrong choice—no exceptions.

—.—.—.—.—.—.—

Sin is largely a matter of mistaken priorities. Any sin in us that is cherished, hidden, and not confessed will cut the nerve center of our faith.

Catherine Marshall

MIRACLES GREAT AND SMALL

For nothing will be impossible with God.

Luke 1:37 Holman CSB

God is a miracle worker. Throughout history He has intervened in the course of human events in ways that cannot be explained by science or human rationale. And He's still doing so today.

God's miracles are not limited to special occasions, nor are they witnessed by a select few. God is crafting His wonders all around us: the miracle of the birth of a new baby; the miracle of a world renewing itself with every sunrise; the miracle of lives transformed by God's love and grace. Each day, God's handiwork is evident for all to see and experience.

Today, seize the opportunity to inspect God's hand at work. His miracles come in a variety of shapes and sizes, so keep your eyes and your heart open. Be watchful, and you'll soon be amazed.

—.—.—.—.—.—.—.—

Are you looking for a miracle? If you keep your eyes wide open and trust in God, you won't have to look very far.

Marie T. Freeman

A CHANGE OF HEART

He who conceals his sins does not prosper, but whoever confesses and renounces them finds mercy.

Proverbs 28:13 NIV

Who among us has sinned? All of us. But, God calls upon us to turn away from sin by following His commandments. And the good news is this: When we do ask God's forgiveness and turn our hearts to Him, He forgives us absolutely and completely.

Genuine repentance requires more than simply offering God apologies for our misdeeds. Real repentance may start with feelings of sorrow and remorse, but it ends only when we turn away from the sin that has heretofore distanced us from our Creator. In truth, we offer our most meaningful apologies to God, not with our words, but with our actions. As long as we are still engaged in sin, we may be "repenting," but we have not fully "repented."

Is there an aspect of your life that is distancing you from your God? If so, ask for His forgiveness, and—just as importantly—stop sinning. Then, wrap yourself in the protection of God's Word. When you do, you will be secure.

—.—.—.—.—.—.—

God sees everything we've ever done and He's willing to forgive. But we must confess to him.

Ruth Bell Graham

SMALL ACTS OF KINDNESS

I tell you the truth, whatever you did for one of the least of these brothers of mine, you did for me.

Matthew 25:40 NIV

Kindness is a choice. Sometimes, when we feel happy or generous, we find it easy to be kind. Other times, when we are discouraged or tired, we can scarcely summon the energy to utter a single kind word. But, God's commandment is clear: He intends that we make the conscious choice to treat others with kindness and respect, no matter our circumstances, no matter our emotions.

In the busyness and confusion of daily life, it is easy to lose focus, and it is easy to become frustrated. We are imperfect human beings struggling to manage our lives as best we can, but we often fall short. When we are distracted or disappointed, we may neglect to share a kind word or a kind deed. This oversight hurts others, but it hurts us most of all.

Today, slow yourself down and be alert for people who need your smile, your kind words, or your helping hand. Make kindness a centerpiece of your dealings with others. They will be blessed, and you will be, too.

MISTAKES: THE PRICE OF BEING HUMAN

Lord, help! they cried in their trouble, and he saved them from their distress.

Psalm 107:13 NLT

Mistakes: nobody likes 'em but everybody makes 'em. Sometimes, even if you're a very good person, you're going to mess things up. And when you do, God is always ready to forgive you—He'll do His part, but you should be willing to do your part, too. Here's what you need to do:

1. If you've been engaging in behavior that is against the will of God, cease and desist (that means stop). 2. If you made a mistake, learn from it and don't repeat it (that's called getting smarter). 3. If you've hurt somebody, apologize and ask for forgiveness (that's called doing the right thing). 4. Ask for God's forgiveness, too (He'll give it whenever you ask, but you do need to ask!). Have you made a mistake? If so, today is the perfect day to make things right with everybody (and the word "everybody" includes yourself, your family, your friends, and your God).

Mistakes are the price you pay for being human; repeated mistakes are the price you pay for being stubborn. So don't be hardheaded: learn from your experiences—the first time!

THE PLAN ACCORDING TO GOD

I will instruct you and teach you in the way you should go; I will guide you with My eye.

Psalm 32:8 NKJV

Perhaps you have a clearly defined plan for the future, but even if you don't, rest assured that God does. God's has a definite plan for every aspect of your life. Your challenge is straightforward: to sincerely pray for God's guidance, and to obediently follow the guidance you receive.

If you're burdened by the demands of everyday life here in the 21st century, you are not alone. Life is difficult at times, and uncertain. But of this you can be sure: God has a plan for you and yours. He will communicate His plans using the Holy Spirit, His Holy Word, and your own conscience. So listen to God's voice and be watchful for His signs: He will send you messages every day of your life, including this one. Your job is to listen, to learn, to trust, and to act.

—.—.—.—.—.—.—.—

Plan ahead—it wasn't raining when Noah built the ark.

Anonymous

ETERNAL LIFE: GOD'S PRICELESS GIFT

I have written these things to you who believe in the name of the Son of God, so that you may know that you have eternal life.

1 John 5:13 Holman CSB

Eternal life is not an event that begins when you die. Eternal life begins when you invite Jesus into your heart right here on earth. So it's important to remember that God's plans for you are not limited to the ups and downs of everyday life. If you've allowed Jesus to reign over your heart, you've already begun your eternal journey.

As mere mortals, our vision for the future, like our lives here on earth, is limited. God's vision is not burdened by such limitations: His plans extend throughout all eternity.

Let us praise the Creator for His priceless gift, and let us share the Good News with all who cross our paths. We return our Father's love by accepting His grace and by sharing His message and His love. When we do, we are blessed here on earth and throughout all eternity.

—·—·—·—·—·—·—

God loves you and wants you to experience peace and life—abundant and eternal.

Billy Graham

OUR FAMILIES ARE WATCHING

You must choose for yourselves today whom you will serve . . . as for me and my family, we will serve the Lord.

Joshua 24:15 NCV

How do people know that you're a Christian? Well, you can tell them, of course. And make no mistake about it: talking about your faith in God is a very good thing to do. But simply telling people about Jesus isn't enough. You must also be willing to show people how a radical Christian (like you) should behave.

Jesus never comes "next." He is always first. And, if you seek to follow Him, you must do so every day of the week, not just on Sundays. After all, you are indeed "the light that gives light to the world," and shouldn't your light shine all the time? Of course it should. God deserves no less, and neither, for that matter, do you.

—.—.—.—.—.—

The secret of a happy home life is that the members of the family learn to give and receive love.

Billy Graham

POSSESSED BY FAITH

The Good News shows how God makes people right with himself—that it begins and ends with faith. As the Scripture says, "But those who are right with God will live by trusting in him."

Romans 1:17 NCV

Can you honestly say that you are an enthusiastic believer? Are you passionate about your faith and excited about your path? Hopefully so. But if your zest for life has waned, it is now time to redirect your efforts and recharge your spiritual batteries. And that means refocusing your priorities by putting God first.

Nothing is more important than your wholehearted commitment to your Creator and to His only begotten Son. Your faith must never be an afterthought; it must be your ultimate priority, your ultimate possession, and your ultimate passion.

—.—.—.—.—.—

When we realize and embrace the Lord's will for us, we will love to do it. We won't want to do anything else. It's a passion.

Franklin Graham

TIME: THE FABRIC OF LIFE

Lord, tell me when the end will come and how long I will live. Let me know how long I have. You have given me only a short life . . . . Everyone's life is only a breath.

Psalm 39:4–5 NCV

Every day, like every life, is composed of moments. Each moment of your life holds within it the potential to seek God's will and to serve His purposes. If you are wise, you will strive to do both.

An important part of wisdom is the wise use of time. How will you invest your time today? Will you savor the moments of your life, or will you squander them? Will you use your time as an instrument of God's will, or will you allow commonplace distractions to rule your day and your life?

The gift of time is a gift from God. Treat it as if it were a precious, fleeting, one-of-a-kind treasure. Because it is.

—·—·—·—·—·—·—

There were endless demands on Jesus' time. Still he was able to make that amazing claim of "completing the work you gave me to do." (John 17:4 NIV)

Elisabeth Elliot

MAKING THE MOST OF OUR TALENTS

Do not neglect the spiritual gift that is within you . . . .

1 Timothy 4:14 NASB

Face it: you've got an array of talents that need to be refined. All people possess special gifts—bestowed from the Father above—and you are no exception. But, your gift is no guarantee of success; it must be cultivated—by you—or it will go unused . . . and God's gift to you will be squandered.

Today, make a promise to yourself that you will earnestly seek to discover the talents that God has given you. Then, nourish those talents and make them grow. Finally, vow to share your gifts with the world for as long as God gives you the power to do so. After all, the best way to say "Thank You" for God's gifts is to use them.

—.—.—.—.—.—.—

Not everyone possesses boundless energy or a conspicuous talent. We are not equally blessed with great intellect or physical beauty or emotional strength. But we have all been given the same ability to be faithful.

Gigi Graham Tchividjian

WORDS WORTHY OF OUR SAVIOR

No rotten talk should come from your mouth, but only what is good for the building up of someone in need, in order to give grace to those who hear.

Ephesians 4:29 Holman CSB

Are you a person who consistently strives to speak words that are pleasing to God? Hopefully so. If you genuinely desire to be godly, your words and your actions must demonstrate your faithfulness to the Creator.

Today, as you fulfill the responsibilities that God has placed before you, ask yourself this question: "Do my words and deeds bear witness to the ultimate Truth that God has placed in my heart, or am I allowing the pressures of everyday life to overwhelm me?" It's a profound question that only you can answer.

Of course you must never take the Lord's name in vain, but it doesn't stop there. You must also strive to speak words of encouragement, words that lift others up, words that give honor to your Heavenly Father.

The Bible clearly warns that you will be judged by the words you speak, so choose those words carefully. And remember: God is always listening.

A NEW DAY, A NEW PATH

Now that you are obedient children of God do not live as you did in the past. You did not understand, so you did the evil things you wanted. But be holy in all you do, just as God, the One who called you, is holy.

1 Peter 1:14–15 NCV

How will you respond to Christ's sacrifice? Will you take up His cross and follow Him (Luke 9:23), or will you choose another path? When you place your hopes squarely at the foot of the cross, when you place Jesus squarely at the center of your life, you will be blessed.

The 19th-century writer Hannah Whitall Smith observed, "The crucial question for each of us is this: What do you think of Jesus, and do you yet have a personal acquaintance with Him?" Indeed, the answer to that question determines the quality, the course, and the direction of our lives today and for all eternity.

Let us put down our old ways and pick up His cross. Let us walk the path that He walked.

—.—.—.—.—.—.—

Christ is not valued at all unless He is valued above all.

St. Augustine

CHRISTIANITY HERE AND NOW

Teach me to do Your will, for You are my God; Your Spirit is good. Lead me in the land of uprightness.

Psalm 143:10 NKJV

Jesus made an extreme sacrifice for you. Are you willing to make extreme changes in your life for Him? Can you honestly say that you're passionate about your faith and that you're really following Jesus? Hopefully so. But if you're preoccupied with other things—or if you're strictly a one-day-a-week Christian—then you're in need of an extreme spiritual makeover!

Jesus doesn't want you to be a run-of-the-mill, follow-the-crowd kind of girl. Jesus wants you to be a "new creation" through Him. And that's exactly what you should want for yourself, too. Nothing is more important than your wholehearted commitment to your Creator and to His only begotten Son. Your faith must never be an afterthought; it must be your ultimate priority, your ultimate possession, and your ultimate passion.

You are the recipient of Christ's love. Accept it enthusiastically and share it passionately. Jesus deserves your extreme enthusiasm; the world deserves it; and you deserve the experience of sharing it.

EXPECTING GOD'S BLESSINGS

*My cup runs over. Surely goodness and mercy shall
follow me all the days of my life; and I will dwell in the
house of the Lord forever.*

Psalm 23:5-6 NKJV

Face facts: Pessimism and Christianity don't mix.
Why? Because Christians have every reason to be
optimistic about life here on earth and life eternal. Mrs.
Charles E. Cowman advised, "Never yield to gloomy
anticipation. Place your hope and confidence in God.
He has no record of failure."

Sometimes, despite our trust in God, we may fall
into the spiritual traps of worry, frustration, anxiety, or
sheer exhaustion, and our hearts become heavy. What's
needed is plenty of rest, a large dose of perspective, and
God's healing touch, but not necessarily in that order.

Today, make this promise to yourself and keep it: vow
to be a hope-filled Christian. Think optimistically about
your life, your education, your family, and your future.
Trust your hopes, not your fears. Take time to celebrate
God's glorious creation. And then, when you've filled
your heart with hope, share your optimism with others.
They'll be better for it, and so will you. But not necessarily
in that order.

ANSWERED PRAYERS

God answered their prayers because they trusted him.

1 Chronicles 5:20 MSG

God answers our prayers. What God does not do is this: He does not answer our prayers in a time and fashion of our choosing, and He does not always answer our prayers in the affirmative. Sometimes our loving Heavenly Father responds to our requests by saying "No," and we must accept His answer, even though we may not understand it.

God answers prayers not according to our wishes but according to His master plan. We cannot know that plan, but we can know the Planner . . . and we must trust His wisdom, His righteousness, and His unending love.

—.—.—.—.—.—.—

What God gives in answer to our prayers will always be the thing we most urgently need, and it will always be sufficient.

Elisabeth Elliot

EARTHLY PRESSURES AND THE SPIRITUAL PATH

See, we count as blessed those who have endured. You have heard of Job's endurance and have seen the outcome from the Lord: the Lord is very compassionate and merciful.

James 5:11 Holman CSB

Some friends encourage us to obey God—these friends help us make wise choices. Other friends put us in situations where we are tempted to disobey God—these friends tempt us to make unwise choices.

Are you hanging out with people who make you a better Christian, or are you spending time with people who encourage you to stray from your faith? The answer to this question will help determine the condition of your spiritual health. One of the best ways to ensure that you follow Christ is to find fellow believers who are willing to follow Him with you.

—.—.—.—.—.—.—

For better or worse, you will eventually become more and more like the people you associate with. So why not associate with people who make you better, not worse?

Marie T. Freeman

LESSONS IN LEADERSHIP

Shepherd God's flock among you, not overseeing out of compulsion but freely, according to God's will; not for the money but eagerly.

1 Peter 5:2 Holman CSB

John Maxwell writes, "Great leaders understand that the right attitude will set the right atmosphere, which enables the right response from others." If you are in a position of leadership, whether at work or at school, it's up to you to set the right tone by maintaining the right attitude.

What's your attitude today? Are you fearful, angry, confused, bitter, or pessimistic? If so, then you should ask yourself if you're the kind of leader whom you would want to follow. If the answer to that question is no, then it's time to improve your leadership skills.

Our world needs Christian leadership. You can become a trusted, competent, thoughtful leader if you learn to maintain the right attitude: one that is realistic, optimistic, forward looking, and Christ-centered.

—·—·—·—·—·—

A true and safe leader is likely to be one who has not desire to lead, but is forced into a position of leadership by inward pressure of the Holy Spirit and the press of external situation.

A. W. Tozer

TRUSTING THE QUIET VOICE

In quietness and trust is your strength.

Isaiah 30:15 NASB

Whenever you're about to make an important decision, you should listen carefully to the quiet voice inside. Sometimes, of course, it's tempting to do otherwise. From time to time, you'll be tempted to abandon your better judgement by ignoring your conscience. Don't do it.

Instead of ignoring that quiet little voice, pay careful attention to it. If you do, your conscience will lead you in the right direction—in fact, it's trying to lead you right now. So listen . . . and learn.

—.—.—.—.—.—.—.—

When we learn to listen to Christ's voice for the details of our daily decisions, we begin to know Him personally.

Catherine Marshall

BEYOND ANGER

Mockers can get a whole town agitated, but those who are wise will calm anger.

Proverbs 29:8 NLT

Your temper is either your master or your servant. Either you control it, or it controls you. And the extent to which you allow anger to rule your life will determine, to a surprising extent, the quality of your relationships with others and your relationship with God.

Anger and peace cannot coexist in the same mind. If you allow yourself to be chronically angry, you must forfeit, albeit temporarily, the peace that might otherwise be yours through Christ. So obey God's Word by turning away from anger today and every day. You'll be glad you did, and so will your family and friends.

—.—.—.—.—.—.—

Anger unresolved will only bring you woe.

Kay Arthur

THE POSSESSIONS WE OWN, AND VICE VERSA

We brought nothing into the world, so we can take nothing out. But, if we have food and clothes, we will be satisfied with that.

1 Timothy 6:7-8 NCV

How important are your material possessions? Not as important as you might think. In the life of a committed Christian, material possessions should play a rather small role. In fact, when we become overly enamored with the things we own, we needlessly distance ourselves from the peace that God offers to those who place Him at the center of their lives.

Of course, we all need the basic necessities of life, but once we meet those needs for ourselves and for our families, the piling up of possessions creates more problems than it solves. Our real riches, of course, are not of this world. We are never really rich until we are rich in spirit.

Do you find yourself wrapped up in the concerns of the material world? If so, it's time to reorder your priorities by turning your thoughts and your prayers to more important matters. And, it's time to begin storing up riches that will endure throughout eternity: the spiritual kind.

DIRECTING OUR THOUGHTS

Finally, brothers, whatever is true, whatever is noble, whatever is right, whatever is pure, whatever is lovely, whatever is admirable—if anything is excellent or praiseworthy—think about such things.

Philippians 4:8 NIV

How will you direct your thoughts today? Will you obey the words of Philippians 4:8 by dwelling upon those things that are honorable, true, and worthy of praise? Or will you allow your thoughts to be hijacked by the negativity that seems to dominate our troubled world?

Are you fearful, angry, bored, or worried? Are you so preoccupied with the concerns of this day that you fail to thank God for the promise of eternity? Are you confused, bitter, or pessimistic? If so, God wants to have a little talk with you. He wants to remind you of His infinite love and His boundless grace. As you contemplate these things, and as you give thanks for God's blessings, negativity should no longer dominate your day or your life.

—.—.—.—.—.—.—

I became aware of one very important concept I had missed before: my attitude—not my circumstances—was what was making me unhappy.

Vonette Bright

GIVING GOD OUR COMPLETE ATTENTION

Worship the Lord your God and . . . serve Him only.

Matthew 4:10 Holman CSB

Nineteenth-century clergyman Edwin Hubbel Chapin warned, "Neutral people are the devil's allies." His words were true then, and they're true now. Neutrality in the face of evil is a sin. Yet all too often, we fail to fight evil, not because we are neutral, but because we are shortsighted: we don't fight the devil because we don't recognize his handiwork.

If we are to recognize evil and fight it, we must pay careful attention. We must pay attention to God's Word, and we must pay attention to the realities of everyday life. When we observe life objectively, and when we do so with eyes and hearts that are attuned to God's Holy Word, we can no longer be neutral believers. And when we are no longer neutral, God rejoices while the devil despairs.

—.—.—.—.—.—.—.—

If you examined a hundred people who had lost their faith in Christianity, I wonder how many of them would turn out to have been reasoned out of it by honest argument? Do not most people simply drift away?

C. S. Lewis

LESSONS IN PATIENCE

Give all your worries and cares to God, for he cares about what happens to you.

1 Peter 5:6 NLT

Sometimes, the hardest thing to do is to wait. After all, most of us are in a hurry for good things to happen. We know what we want and we know when we want it: immediately, if not sooner. Yet God's plans do not always unfold in ways we would prefer or at times of our own choosing. Our task—as believers who trust in a benevolent, all-knowing Father—is to wait patiently for God to reveal Himself.

Are you just a little bit impatient? Are you a get-it-done-now girl who wants things to happen TODAY? If so, you should realize that God has created a world which unfolds according to His own timetable, not yours . . . and God always knows best. So trust His timetable today, tomorrow, and always.

—.—.—.—.—.—

When we read of the great Biblical leaders, we see that it was not uncommon for God to ask them to wait, not just a day or two, but for years, until God was ready for them to act.

Gloria Gaither

A PLAN FOR TODAY

Depend on the Lord in whatever you do, and your plans will succeed.

Proverbs 16:3 NCV

Would you like a formula for successful living that never fails? Here it is: Include God in every aspect of your life's journey, including the plans that you make and the steps that you take. But beware: as you make plans for the days and weeks ahead, you may become sidetracked by the demands of everyday living.

If you allow the world to establish your priorities, you will eventually become discouraged or disappointed, or both. But if you genuinely seek God's will for every important decision that you make, your loving Heavenly Father will guide your steps and enrich your life. So as you plan your work, remember that every good plan should start with God, including yours.

—.—.—.—.—.—.—

You can't start building a better tomorrow if you wait till tomorrow to start building.

Marie T. Freeman

ALONE WITH GOD

Step out of the traffic! Take a long, loving look at me, your High God, above politics, above everything

Psalm 46:10 MSG

As you organize your day and your life, where does God fit in? Do you "squeeze Him in" on Sundays and at mealtimes? Or do you consult Him more often than that?

This book asks that you give your undivided attention to God for at least two minutes each day. And make no mistake about it: the emphasis in the previous sentence should be placed on the words "at least." In truth, you should give God lots more time than a couple of minutes a day, but hey, it's a start.

Even if you're the busiest person on the planet, you can still carve out a little time for God. And when you think about it, isn't that the very least you should do?

—.—.—.—.—.—.—

How motivating it has been for me to view my early morning devotions as time of retreat alone with Jesus, Who desires that I "come with Him by myself to a quiet place" in order to pray, read His Word, listen for His voice, and be renewed in my spirit.

Anne Graham Lotz

RENEWAL DAY BY DAY

So we're not giving up. How could we! Even though on the outside it often looks like things are falling apart on us, on the inside, where God is making new life, not a day goes by without his unfolding grace.

2 Corinthians 4:16 MSG

God's Word is clear: When we genuinely lift our hearts and prayers to Him, He renews our strength. Are you almost too weary to lift your head? Then bow it. Offer your concerns and your fears to your Father in heaven. He is always at your side, offering His love and His strength.

Are you troubled or anxious? Take your anxieties to God in prayer. Are you weak or worried? Delve deeply into God's Holy Word and sense His presence in the quiet moments of the early morning. Are you spiritually exhausted? Call upon fellow believers to support you, and call upon Christ to renew your spirit and your life. Your Savior will not let you down. To the contrary, He will lift you up when you ask Him to do so. So what, dear friend, are you waiting for?

—.—.—.—.—.—

Jesus taught us by example to get out of the rat race and recharge our batteries.

Barbara Johnson

THE HEART OF A THANKFUL CHRISTIAN

In everything give thanks; for this is the will of God in Christ Jesus for you.

2 Thessalonians 5:18 NKJV

As believing Christians, we are blessed beyond measure. God sent His only Son to die for our sins. And, God has given us the priceless gifts of eternal love and eternal life. We, in turn, are instructed to approach our Heavenly Father with reverence and thanksgiving. But sometimes, in the crush of everyday living, we simply don't stop long enough to pause and thank our Creator for the countless blessings He has bestowed upon us.

When we slow down and express our gratitude to the One who made us, we enrich our own lives and the lives of those around us. Thanksgiving should become a habit, a regular part of our daily routines. God has blessed us beyond measure, and we owe Him everything, including our eternal praise. To paraphrase the familiar children's blessing, "God is great, God is good, let us thank Him for . . . everything!"

—.—.—.—.—.—.—.—

Words fail to express my love for this holy Book, my gratitude for its author, for His love and goodness. How shall I thank him for it?

Lottie Moon

WISDOM FROM ABOVE

The Lord says, "I will make you wise and show you where to go. I will guide you and watch over you."

Psalm 32:8 NCV

Sometimes, amid the concerns of everyday life, we lose perspective. Life seems out of balance as we confront an array of demands that sap our strength and cloud our thoughts. What's needed is a renewed faith, a fresh perspective, and God's wisdom.

In today's world, commentary is commonplace and information is everywhere. But the ultimate source of wisdom, the kind of timeless wisdom that God willingly shares with His children, is still available from a single unique source: the Holy Bible.

The wisdom of the world changes with the ever-shifting sands of public opinion. God's wisdom does not. His wisdom is eternal. It never changes. And it most certainly is the wisdom that you must use to plan your day, your life, and your eternal destiny.

—·—·—·—·—·—·—

If we neglect the Bible, we cannot expect to benefit from the wisdom and direction that result from knowing God's Word.

Vonette Bright

CONTAGIOUS CHRISTIANITY

All those who stand before others and say they believe in me, I will say before my Father in heaven that they belong to me.

Matthew 10:32 NCV

Genuine, heartfelt Christianity is contagious. If you enjoy a life-altering relationship with God, that relationship will have an impact on others—perhaps a profound impact.

Are you genuinely excited about your faith? And do you make your enthusiasm known to those around you? Or are you a "silent ambassador" for Christ? God's preference is clear: He intends that you stand before others and proclaim your faith.

Does Christ reign over your life? Then share your testimony and your excitement. The world needs both.

—.—.—.—.—.—.—

Christians are like coals of a fire. Together they glow—apart they grow cold.

Anonymous

ABANDONING THE STATUS QUO

I have come as a light into the world, so that everyone who believes in Me would not remain in darkness.

John 12:46 Holman CSB

Okay, answer this question honestly: Do you behave differently because of your relationship with Jesus? Or do you behave in pretty much the same way that you would if you weren't a believer? Hopefully, the fact that you've invited Christ to reign over your heart means that you've made BIG changes in your thoughts and your actions.

Doing the right thing is not always easy, especially when you're tired or frustrated. But, doing the wrong thing almost always leads to trouble. And sometimes, it leads to big trouble.

If you're determined to follow "the crowd," you may soon find yourself headed in the wrong direction. So here's some advice: Don't follow the crowd—follow Jesus. And keep following Him every day of your life.

—.—.—.—.—.—.—

Will you, with a glad and eager surrender, hand yourself and all that concerns you over into his hands? If you will do this, your soul will begin to know something of the joy of union with Christ.

Hannah Whitall Smith

GROWING WITH AND BEYOND OUR TROUBLES

We also have joy with our troubles, because we know that these troubles produce patience. And patience produces character, and character produces hope.

Romans 5:3-4 NCV

The times that try your soul are also the times that build your character. During the darker days of life, you can learn lessons that are impossible to learn during sunny, happier days. Times of adversity can—and should—be times of intense spiritual and personal growth. But God will not force you to learn the lessons of adversity. You must learn them for yourself.

The next time Old Man Trouble knocks on your door, remember that he has lessons to teach. So turn away Mr. Trouble as quickly as you can, but as you're doing so, don't forget to learn his lessons. And remember that the trouble with trouble isn't just the trouble it causes; it's also the trouble we cause ourselves if we ignore the things that trouble has to teach. Got that? Then please don't forget it!

—.—.—.—.—.—.—.—

Often, our character is at greater risk in prosperity than in adversity.

Beth Moore

VIGILANT CHRISTIANITY

Be careful! Watch out for attacks from the Devil, your great enemy. He prowls around like a roaring lion, looking for some victim to devour. Take a firm stand against him, and be strong in your faith.

1 Peter 5:8-9 NLT

If you stop to think about it, the cold, hard evidence is right in front of your eyes: you live in a temptation-filled world. The devil is out on the street, hard at work, causing pain and heartache in more ways than ever before. Yep, you live in a temptation nation, a place where the bad guys are working 24/7 to lead you astray. That's why you must remain vigilant. Not only must you resist Satan when he confronts you, but you must also avoid those places where Satan can most easily tempt you.

In a letter to believers, Peter offers a stern warning: "Your adversary, the devil, prowls around like a roaring lion, seeking someone to devour" (1 Peter 5:8 NASB). What was true in New Testament times is equally true in our own. Satan tempts his prey and then devours them (and it's up to you—and only you—to make sure that you're not one of the ones being devoured!).

As believing Christians, we must beware because temptations are everywhere. Satan is determined to win; we must be equally determined that he does not.

A WORLD FULL OF PROMISES

For everyone born of God overcomes the world. This is the victory that has overcome the world, even our faith.

1 John 5:4 NIV

The world makes promises that it simply cannot fulfill. It promises happiness, contentment, prosperity, and abundance. But genuine, lasting abundance is not a function of worldly possessions, it is a function of our thoughts, our actions, and the relationship we choose to create with our God. The world's promises are incomplete and illusory; God's promises are unfailing.

We must build our lives on the firm foundation of God's promises . . . nothing else will suffice.

—.—.—.—.—.—.—

All those who look to draw their satisfaction from the wells of the world—pleasure, popularity, position, possessions, politics, power, prestige, finances, family, friends, fame, fortune, career, children, church, clubs, sports, sex, success, recognition, reputation, religion, education, entertainment, exercise, honors, health, hobbies—will soon be thirsty again!

Anne Graham Lotz

OBEDIENCE TO THE ULTIMATE AUTHORITY

We must obey God rather than men.

Acts 5:29 NASB

Obedience to God is determined not by words, but by deeds. Talking about righteousness is easy; living righteously is far more difficult, especially in today's fast-paced, temptation-filled world.

Since God created Adam and Eve, we human beings have been rebelling against our Creator. Why? Because we are unwilling to trust God's Word, and we are unwilling to follow His commandments. God has given us a guidebook for righteous living called the Holy Bible. It contains thorough instructions which, if followed, lead to fulfillment, righteousness, and salvation. But, if we choose to ignore God's commandments, the results are as predictable as they are tragic.

Unless we are willing to abide by God's laws, all of our righteous proclamations ring hollow. How can we best proclaim our love for the Lord? By obeying Him.

—.—.—.—.—.—.—.—

Perfect obedience would be perfect happiness, if only we had perfect confidence in the power we were obeying.

Corrie ten Boom

GUIDED BY HONESTY

Good people will be guided by honesty; dishonesty will destroy those who are not trustworthy.

Proverbs 11:3 NCV

It has been said on many occasions and in many ways that honesty is the best policy. For believers, it is far more important to note that honesty is God's policy. And if we are to be servants worthy of our Savior, Jesus Christ, we must be honest and forthright in our communications with others.

Sometimes, honesty is difficult; sometimes, honesty is painful; always, honesty is God's commandment. In the Book of Exodus, God did not command, "Thou shalt not bear false witness when it is convenient." And He didn't say, "Thou shalt not bear false witness most of the time." God said, "Thou shalt not bear false witness against thy neighbor." Period.

Sometime soon, perhaps even today, you will be tempted to bend the truth or perhaps even to break it. Resist that temptation. Truth is God's way . . . and it must also be yours. Period.

—.—.—.—.—.—.—

God never called us to naïveté. He called us to integrity . . . . The biblical concept of integrity emphasizes mature innocence not childlike ignorance.

Beth Moore

SINCE TOMORROW IS NOT PROMISED

We must do the works of Him who sent Me while it is day. Night is coming when no one can work.

John 9:4 Holman CSB

The words of John 9:4 remind us that "night is coming" for all of us. But until then, God gives us each day and fills it to the brim with possibilities. The day is presented to us fresh and clean at midnight, free of charge, but we must beware: Today is a non-renewable resource— once it's gone, it's gone forever. Our responsibility, of course, is to use this day in the service of God's will and in accordance with His commandments.

Today, treasure the time that God has given you. And search for the hidden possibilities that God has placed along your path. This day is a priceless gift from your Creator, so use it joyfully and productively. And encourage others to do likewise.

—.—.—.—.—.—.—

How much of our lives are, well, so daily. How often our hours are filled with the mundane, seemingly unimportant things that have to be done, whether at home or work. These very "daily" tasks could become a celebration of praise. "It is through consecration," someone has said, "that drudgery is made divine."

Gigi Graham Tchividjian

THE RICH HARVEST

Now this I say, he who sows sparingly will also reap sparingly, and he who sows bountifully will also reap bountifully.

2 Corinthians 9:6 NASB

How can we serve God? By sharing His message, His mercy, and His love with those who cross our paths. Everywhere we look, or so it seems, the needs are great. And at every turn, it seems, so are the temptations. Still, our challenge is clear: we must love God, obey His commandments, trust His Son, and serve His children. When we place the Lord in His rightful place—at the center of our lives—we will reap a bountiful spiritual harvest that will endure forever.

—.—.—.—.—.—.—

That's what I love about serving God. In His eyes, there are no little people . . . because there are no big people. We are all on the same playing field.

Joni Eareckson Tada

QUIET, PLEASE!

Truly my soul silently waits for God; from Him comes my salvation.

Psalm 62:1 NKJV

Face it: We live in a noisy world, a world filled with distractions, frustrations, and complications. But if we allow those distractions to separate us from God's peace, we do ourselves a profound disservice.

Are you one of those who rush through the day with scarcely a single moment for quiet contemplation and prayer? If so, it's time to reorder your priorities.

Nothing is more important than the time you spend with your Savior. So be still and claim the inner peace that is your spiritual birthright: the peace of Jesus Christ. It is offered freely; it has been paid for in full; it is yours for the asking. So ask. And then share.

—.—.—.—.—.—.—

If you, too, will learn to wait upon God, to get alone with Him, and remain silent so that you can hear His voice when He is ready to speak to you, what a difference it will make in your life!

Kay Arthur

SELECTING YOUR ROADMAP

Teach me, O Lord, the way of Your statutes, and I shall keep it to the end.

Psalm 119:33 NKJV

As you look to the future and decide upon the direction of your life, what will you use as your roadmap? Will you trust God's Holy Word and use it as an indispensable tool to guide your steps? Or will you choose a different map to guide your steps? The map you choose will determine the quality of your journey and its ultimate destination.

The Bible is the ultimate guide for life; make it your guidebook as well. When you do, you can be comforted in the knowledge that your steps are guided by a Source of wisdom and truth that never fails.

—.—.—.—.—.—.—

Brother, is your faith looking upward today? Trust in the promise of the Savior. Sister, is the light shining bright on your way? Trust in the promise of thy Lord.

Fanny Crosby

STEWARDSHIP OF YOUR TIME

Teach us to number our days carefully so that we may develop wisdom in our hearts.

Psalm 90:12 Holman CSB

Time is a nonrenewable gift from God. But sometimes, we treat our time here on earth as if it were not a gift at all: We may be tempted to invest our lives in trivial pursuits and petty diversions. But our Father beckons each of us to a higher calling.

An important element of our stewardship to God is the way we choose to spend the time He has entrusted to us. Each waking moment holds the potential to do a good deed, to say a kind word, or to offer a heartfelt prayer. Our challenge, as believers, is to use our time wisely in the service of God's work and in accordance with His plan for our lives.

Each day is a special treasure to be savored and celebrated. May we—as Christians who have so much to celebrate—never fail to praise our Creator by rejoicing in this glorious day, and by using it wisely.

—.—.—.—.—.—.—

Frustration is not the will of God. There is time to do anything and everything that God wants us to do.

Elisabeth Elliot

A GOD OF POSSIBILITIES

Jesus looked at them and said, "With man this is impossible, but with God all things are possible."

Matthew 19:26 NIV

If you really want to know God, you must be willing to worship Him seven days a week, not just on Sunday.

God has a wonderful plan for your life, and an important part of that plan includes the time that you set aside for praise and worship. Every life, including yours, is based upon some form of worship. The question is not whether you will worship, but what you worship.

If you choose to worship God, you will receive a bountiful harvest of joy, peace, and abundance. But if you distance yourself from God by foolishly worshiping earthly possessions and personal gratification, you're making a huge mistake. So do this: Worship God today and every day. Worship Him with sincerity and thanksgiving. Write His name on your heart and rest assured that He, too, has written your name on His.

—.—.—.—.—. • —.—.—

To worship Him in truth means to worship Him honestly, without hypocrisy, standing open and transparent before Him.

Anne Graham Lotz

THE REWARDS OF RIGHTEOUSNESS

Test all things; hold fast what is good. Abstain from every form of evil.

1 Thessalonians 5:21-22 NKJV

When we seek righteousness in our own lives—and when we seek the companionship of those who do likewise—we reap the spiritual rewards that God intends for us to enjoy. When we behave ourselves as godly men and women, we honor God. When we live righteously and according to God's commandments, He blesses us in ways that we cannot fully understand.

Today, as you fulfill your responsibilities, hold fast to that which is good, and associate yourself with believers who behave themselves in like fashion. When you do, your good works will serve as a powerful example for others and as a worthy offering to your Creator.

—.—.—.—.—.—.—

Let us never suppose that obedience is impossible or that holiness is meant only for a select few. Our Shepherd leads us in paths of righteousness—not for our name's sake but for His.

Elisabeth Elliot

PRAYERFUL HEARTS AND WILLING HANDS

So you may walk in the way of goodness, and keep to the paths of righteousness. For the upright will dwell in the land, And the blameless will remain in it.

Proverbs 2:20-21 NKJV

The old adage is both familiar and true: We must pray as if everything depended upon God, but work as if everything depended upon us. Yet sometimes, when we are weary and discouraged, we may allow our worries to sap our energy and our hope. God has other intentions. God intends that we pray for things, and He intends that we be willing to work for the things that we pray for. More importantly, God intends that our work should become His work.

Are you willing to work diligently for yourself and for your God? And are you willing to engage in work that is pleasing to your Creator? If so, you can expect your Heavenly Father to bring forth a rich harvest.

And if you have concerns about the inevitable challenges of everyday living, take those concerns to God in prayer. He will guide your steps, He will steady your hand, He will calm your fears, and He will reward your efforts.

QUIET CHARITY

Be careful not to do your acts of righteousness before men, to be seen by them. If you do, you will have no reward from your Father in heaven.

Matthew 6:1 NIV

Hymn writer Fanny Crosby wrote, "To God be the glory; great thing He hath done!" But sometimes, because we are imperfect human beings, we seek the glory. Sometimes, when we do good deeds, we seek to glorify our achievements in a vain attempt to build ourselves up in the eyes of our neighbors. To do so is a profound mistake.

God's Word gives specific instructions about how we should approach our acts of charity: The glory must go to God, not to us. All praise belongs to the Giver of all good gifts: our Father in heaven. We are simply conduits for His generosity, and we must remain humble . . . extremely humble.

—.—.—.—.—.—.—

The measure of a life, after all, is not its duration but its donation.

Corrie ten Boom

OUR PURPOSES, GOD'S PURPOSES

For we are His making, created in Christ Jesus for good works, which God prepared ahead of time so that we should walk in them.

Ephesians 2:10 Holman CSB

Whenever we struggle against God's plans, we suffer. When we resist God's calling, our efforts bear little fruit. Our best strategy, therefore, is to seek God's wisdom and to follow Him wherever He chooses to lead. When we do so, we are blessed.

When we align ourselves with God's purposes, we avail ourselves of His power and His peace. But how can we know precisely what God's intentions are? The answer, of course, is that even the most well-intentioned believers face periods of uncertainty and doubt about the direction of their lives. So, too, will you.

When you arrive at one of life's inevitable crossroads, that is precisely the moment when you should turn your thoughts and prayers toward God. When you do, He will make Himself known to you in a time and manner of His choosing.

—·—·—·—·—·—

God will help us become the people we are meant to be, if only we will ask Him.

Hannah Whitall Smith

THE SEARCH FOR WISDOM

If you don't know what you're doing, pray to the Father. He loves to help. You'll get his help, and won't be condescended to when you ask for it. Ask boldly, believingly, without a second thought. People who "worry their prayers" are like wind-whipped waves. Don't think you're going to get anything from the Master that way, adrift at sea, keeping all your options open.

James 1:5-8 MSG

Do you seek the wisdom that only God can give? If so, ask Him for it! If you ask God for guidance, He will not withhold it. If you petition Him sincerely, and if you genuinely seek to form a relationship with Him, your Heavenly Father will guide your steps and enlighten your heart. But be forewarned: You will not acquire God's wisdom without obeying His commandments. Why? Because God's wisdom is more than just a collection of thoughts; it is, first and foremost, a way of life.

Wisdom is as wisdom does. So if you sincerely seek God's wisdom, don't be satisfied to learn something; make up your mind to become something. And then, as you allow God to remake you in the image of His Son, you will most surely become wise.

—·—·—·—·—·—

"Born Again" doesn't mean "Born Yesterday."

Anonymous

GIVING AN ACCOUNT OF OURSELVES

Yes, each of us will have to give a personal account to God.

Romans 14:12 NLT

For most of us, it is a daunting thought: one day, perhaps soon, we'll come face-to-face with our Heavenly Father, and we'll be called to account for our actions here on earth. Our personal histories will certainly not be surprising to God; He already knows everything about us. But the full scope of our activities may be surprising to us: some of us will be pleasantly surprised; others will not be.

Today, do whatever you can to ensure that your thoughts and your deeds are pleasing to your Creator. Because you will, at some point in the future, be called to account for your actions. And the future may be sooner than you think.

—.—.—.—.—.—.—.—

Don't worry about what you do not understand. Worry about what you do understand in the Bible but do not live by.

Corrie ten Boom

THE TIME TO PLANT SEEDS

Those who wait for perfect weather will never plant seeds; those who look at every cloud will never harvest crops . . . . Plant early in the morning, and work until evening, because you don't know if this or that will succeed. They might both do well.

Ecclesiastes 11:4,6 NCV

Once the season for planting is upon us, the time to plant seeds is when we make time to plant seeds. And when it comes to planting God's seeds in the soil of eternity, the only certain time that we have is now. Yet because we are fallible human beings with limited vision and misplaced priorities, we may be tempted to delay.

If we hope to reap a bountiful harvest for God, for our families, and for ourselves, we must plant now by defeating a dreaded human frailty: the habit of procrastination. Procrastination often results from our shortsighted attempts to postpone temporary discomfort.

A far better strategy is this: Whatever "it" is, do it now. When you do, you won't have to worry about "it" later.

—.—.—.—.—.—.—

We spend our lives dreaming of the future, not realizing that a little of it slips away every day.

Barbara Johnson

WHAT WE BELIEVE AND HOW WE BEHAVE

Not everyone who says to me, "Lord, Lord," will enter the kingdom of heaven, but only he who does the will of my Father who is in heaven.

Matthew 7:21 NIV

In describing one's beliefs, actions are far better descriptors than words. Yet far too many of us spend more energy talking about our beliefs than living by them—with predictable consequences.

Is your life a picture book of your creed? Are your actions congruent with your beliefs? Are you willing to practice the philosophy that you preach?

Today and every day, make certain that your actions are guided by God's Word and by the conscience that He has placed in your heart. Don't treat your faith as if it were separate from your everyday life. Weave your beliefs into the very fabric of your day. When you do, God will honor your good works, and your good works will honor God.

—.—.—.—.—.—.—

The mind is a faculty, and magnificent one at that. But the heart is the dwelling place of our true beliefs.

John Eldredge

SPIRITUAL MATURITY, DAY BY DAY

When I was a child, I spoke and thought and reasoned as a child does. But when I grew up, I put away childish things.

1 Corinthians 13:11 NLT

The path to spiritual maturity unfolds day by day. Each day offers the opportunity to worship God, to ignore God, or to rebel against God. When we worship Him with our prayers, our words, our thoughts, and our actions, we are blessed by the richness of our relationship with the Father. But if we ignore God altogether or intentionally rebel against His commandments, we rob ourselves of His blessings.

Today offers yet another opportunity for spiritual growth. If you choose, you can seize that opportunity by obeying God's Word, by seeking His will, and by walking with His Son.

—.—.—.—.—.—.—

God is teaching me to become more and more "teachable": To keep evolving. To keep taking the risk of learning something new . . . or unlearning something old and off base.

Beth Moore

BEYOND STUBBORNNESS

Pride goes before destruction, a haughty spirit before a fall.

Proverbs 16:18 NIV

Since the days of Adam and Eve, human beings have been strong-willed and rebellious. Our rebellion stems, in large part, from an intense desire to do things "our way" instead of "God's way." But when we pridefully choose to forsake God's path for our lives, we do ourselves a sincere injustice . . . and we are penalized because of our stubbornness.

God's Word warns us to be humble, not prideful. God instructs us to be obedient, not rebellious. God wants us to do things His way. When we do, we reap a bountiful harvest of blessings—more blessings than we can count. But when we pridefully rebel against our Creator, we sow the seeds of our own destruction, and we reap a sad, sparse, bitter harvest. May we sow—and reap—accordingly.

—.—.—.—.—.—.—

It was as important to me that my children be no more self-righteous than they were unrighteous. In His Gospels, Christ seemed far more tolerant of a repentant sinner than a self-righteous, self-proclaimed saint.

Beth Moore

THE ART OF GODLY ACCEPTANCE

People may make plans in their minds, but the Lord decides what they will do.

Proverbs 16:9 NCV

Sometimes, we must accept life on its terms, not our own. Life has a way of unfolding, not as we will, but as it will. And sometimes, there is precious little we can do to change things.

When events transpire that are beyond our control, we have a choice: we can either learn the art of acceptance, or we can make ourselves miserable as we struggle to change the unchangeable.

We must entrust the things we cannot change to God. Once we have done so, we can prayerfully and faithfully tackle the important work that He has placed before us: the things we can change.

—·—·—·—·—·—·—

We must meet our disappointments, our persecutions, our malicious enemies, our provoking friends, our trials and temptations of every sort, with an attitude of surrender and trust. We must spread our wings and "mount up" to the "heavenly places in Christ" above them all, where they will lose their power to harm or distress us.

Hannah Whitall Smith

WHEN WE DO OUR PART, GOD DOES HIS

And we know that in all things God works for the good of those who love him, who have been called according to his purpose.

Romans 8:28 NIV

Do the demands of this day threaten to overwhelm you? If so, you must rely not only upon your own resources but also upon the promises of your Father in heaven.

God is a never-ending source of support and courage for those of us who call upon Him. When we are weary, He gives us strength. When we see no hope, God reminds us of His promises. When we grieve, God wipes away our tears.

God will hold your hand and walk with you every day of your life if you let Him. So even if your circumstances are difficult, trust the Father. His love is eternal and His goodness endures forever.

—.—.—.—.—.—

Our helplessness can be a healthy sign. This is always a good place to begin a task that seems completely impossible.

Catherine Marshall

LIFETIME LEARNING

Above all and before all, do this: Get Wisdom! Write this at the top of your list: Get Understanding!

Proverbs 4:7 MSG

Whether you're fifteen or a hundred and fifteen, you've still got lots to learn. Even if you're a very wise person, God isn't finished with you yet. Why? Because lifetime learning is part of God's plan—and He certainly hasn't finished teaching you some very important lessons.

Do you seek to live a life of righteousness and wisdom? If so, you must continue to study the ultimate source of wisdom: the Word of God. You must associate, day in and day out, with godly men and women. And, you must act in accordance with your beliefs. When you study God's Word and live according to His commandments, you will become wise . . . and you will be a blessing to your friends, to your family, and to the world.

—.—.—.—.—.—.—

While chastening is always difficult, if we look to God for the lesson we should learn, we will see spiritual fruit.

Vonette Bright

HABITS THAT ARE PLEASING TO GOD

I the Lord search the heart and examine the mind, to reward a man according to his conduct, according to what his deeds deserve.

Jeremiah 17:10 NIV

It's an old saying and a true one: First, you make your habits, and then your habits make you. Some habits will inevitably bring you closer to God; other habits will lead you away from the path He has chosen for you. If you sincerely desire to improve your spiritual health, you must honestly examine the habits that make up the fabric of your day. And you must abandon those habits that are displeasing to God.

If you trust God, and if you keep asking for His help, He can transform your life. If you sincerely ask Him to help you, the same God who created the universe will help you defeat the harmful habits that have heretofore defeated you. So, if at first you don't succeed, keep praying. God is listening, and He's ready to help you become a better person if you ask Him . . . so ask today.

—.—.—.—.—.—.—

Prayer is a habit. Worship is a habit. Kindness is a habit. And if you want to please God, you'd better make sure that these habits are your habits.

Marie T. Freeman

FOLLOWING HIS FOOTSTEPS

But whoever keeps His word, truly in him the love of God is perfected. This is how we know we are in Him: the one who says he remains in Him should walk just as He walked.

1 John 2:5-6 Holman CSB

Life is a series of choices. Each day, we make countless decisions that can bring us closer to God . . . or not. When we live according to God's commandments, we reap bountiful rewards: abundance, hope, and peace, for starters. But, when we turn our backs upon God by disobeying Him, we bring needless suffering upon ourselves and our families.

Do you seek to walk in the footsteps of the One from Galilee, or will you choose another path? If you sincerely seek God's peace and His blessings, then you must strive to imitate God's Son.

Thomas Brooks spoke for believers of every generation when he observed, "Christ is the sun, and all the watches of our lives should be set by the dial of his motion." Christ, indeed, is the ultimate Savior of mankind and the personal Savior of those who believe in Him. As His servants, we should walk in His footsteps as we share His love and His message with a world that needs both.

AIMING HIGH

I can do everything through him that gives me strength.
Philippians 4:13 NIV

Do you expect your future to be bright? Are you willing to dream king-sized dreams . . . and are you willing to work diligently to make those dreams happen? Hopefully so—after all, God promises that we can do "all things" through Him. Yet most of us, even the most devout among us, live far below our potential. We take half measures; we dream small dreams; we waste precious time and energy on the distractions of the world. But God has other plans for us.

Our Creator intends that we live faithfully, hopefully, courageously, and abundantly. He knows that we are capable of so much more; and He wants us to do the things we're capable of doing; and He wants us to begin doing those things today.

—.—.—.—.—.—.—

The future lies all before us. Shall it only be a slight advance upon what we usually do? Ought it not to be a bound, a leap forward to altitudes of endeavor and success undreamed of before?

Annie Armstrong

THE SOURCE OF STRENGTH

Happy are the people whose strength is in You, whose hearts are set on pilgrimage.

Psalm 84:5 Holman CSB

Have you tapped in to the power of God? Have you turned your life and your heart over to Him, or are you muddling along under your own power? The answer to this question will determine the quality of your life here on earth and the destiny of your life throughout all eternity.

The Bible tells us that we can do all things through the power of our risen Savior, Jesus Christ. But what does the Bible say about our powers outside the will of Christ? The Bible teaches us that "the wages of sin is death" (Romans 6:23). Our challenge, then, is clear: we must place Christ where He belongs: at the very center of our lives. When we do so, we will surely discover that He offers us the strength to live victoriously in this world and eternally in the next.

—.—.—.—.—.—.—

We are never stronger than the moment we admit we are weak.

Beth Moore

THE SEARCH FOR TRUTH

Then you will know the truth, and the truth will set you free.

John 8:32 NIV

The familiar words of John 8:32 remind us that "the truth shall make you free" (NKJV). And St. Augustine had this advice: "Let everything perish! Dismiss these empty vanities! And let us take up the search for the truth."

God is vitally concerned with truth. His Word teaches the truth; His Spirit reveals the truth; His Son leads us to the truth. When we open our hearts to God, and when we allow His Son to rule over our thoughts and our lives, God reveals Himself, and we come to understand the truth about ourselves and the truth about God's gift of grace.

Are you seeking the truth and living by it? Hopefully so. When you do, you'll discover that the truth will indeed set you free, now and forever.

—.—.—.—.—.—.—

The Holy Spirit was given to guide us into all truth, but He doesn't do it all at once.

Elisabeth Elliot

ENCOURAGING WORDS FOR FAMILY AND FRIENDS

Good people's words will help many others.

Proverbs 10:21 NCV

Life is a team sport, and all of us need occasional pats on the back from our teammates. As Christians, we are called upon to spread the Good News of Christ, and we are also called to spread a message of encouragement and hope to the world.

Whether you realize it or not, many people with whom you come in contact every day are in desperate need of a smile or an encouraging word. The world can be a difficult place, and countless friends and family members may be troubled by the challenges of everyday life. Since you don't always know who needs your help, the best strategy is to try to encourage all the people who cross your path. So today, be a world-class source of encouragement to everyone you meet. Never has the need been greater.

—.—.—.—.—.—.—

A single word, if spoken in a friendly spirit, may be sufficient to turn one from dangerous error.

Fanny Crosby

KEEPING PROSPERITY IN PERSPECTIVE

If your wealth increases, don't make it the center of your life.

Psalm 62:10 NLT

In the demanding world in which we live, financial prosperity can be a good thing, but spiritual prosperity is profoundly more important. Yet our society leads us to believe otherwise. The world glorifies material possessions, personal fame, and physical beauty above all else; these things, of course, are totally unimportant to God. God sees the human heart, and that's what is important to Him.

As you establish your priorities for the coming day, remember this: The world will do everything it can to convince you that "things" are important. The world will tempt you to value fortune above faith and possessions above peace. God, on the other hand, will try to convince you that your relationship with Him is all-important. Trust God.

—·—·—·—·—·—·—

Have you prayed about your resources lately? Find out how God wants you to use your time and your money. No matter what it costs, forsake all that is not of God.

Kay Arthur

DISOBEDIENCE EQUALS DISASTER

You must follow the Lord your God and fear Him. You must keep His commands and listen to His voice; you must worship Him and remain faithful to Him.

Deuteronomy 13:4 Holman CSB

As creatures of free will, we may disobey God whenever we choose, but when we do so, we put ourselves and our loved ones in peril. Why? Because disobedience invites disaster. We cannot sin against God without consequence. We cannot live outside His will without injury. We cannot distance ourselves from God without hardening our hearts. We cannot yield to the ever-tempting distractions of our world and, at the same time, enjoy God's peace.

Sometimes, in a futile attempt to justify our behaviors, we make a distinction between "big" sins and "little" ones. To do so is a mistake of "big" proportions. Sins of all shapes and sizes have the power to do us great harm. And in a world where sin is big business, that's certainly a sobering thought.

—.—.—.—.—.—.—

As a child of God, you are no longer a slave to sin.

Kay Arthur

THE WISDOM OF RIGHTEOUSNESS

A fool finds pleasure in evil conduct, but a man of understanding delights in wisdom.

Proverbs 10:23 NIV

Are you a radically different person because of your decision to form a personal relationship with Jesus? Has Jesus made a BIG difference in your life, or are you basically the same person you were before you invited Him into your heart? The answer to these questions will determine the quality and the direction of your life.

If you're still doing all the same things you did before you became a Christian, it may be time to take an honest look at the current condition of your faith. Why? Because Jesus doesn't want you to be a run-of-the-mill, follow-the-crowd kind of girl. Jesus wants you to be a "new creation" through Him. And that's exactly what you should want for yourself, too.

—.—.—.—.—.—.—

Study the Bible and observe how the persons behaved and how God dealt with them. There is explicit teaching on every condition of life.

Corrie ten Boom

FINDING YOUR WAY

In all your ways acknowledge him, and he will make your paths straight.

Proverbs 3:6 NIV

Proverbs 3:6 makes this promise: if you acknowledge God's sovereignty over every aspect of your life, He will guide your path. And, as you prayerfully consider the path that God intends for you to take, here are things you should do: You should study His Word and be ever-watchful for His signs. You should associate with fellow believers who will encourage your spiritual growth. You should listen carefully to that inner voice that speaks to you in the quiet moments of your daily devotionals. And, as you continually seek God's unfolding purpose for your life, you should be patient. Your Heavenly Father may not always reveal Himself as quickly as you would like. But rest assured: God is here, and He intends to use you in wonderful, unexpected ways. He desires to lead you along a path of His choosing. Your challenge is to watch, to listen, to learn . . . and to follow.

—.—.—.—.—.—.—

Only God's chosen task for you will ultimately satisfy. Do not wait until it is too late to realize the privilege of serving Him in His chosen position for you.

Beth Moore

WHEN WE STUMBLE

God is our refuge and strength, always ready to help in times of trouble. So we will not fear, even if earthquakes come and mountains crumble to the sea.

Psalm 46:1-2 NLT

From time to time, all of us face adversity, discouragement, or disappointment. And, throughout life, we must all endure life-changing personal losses that leave us breathless. When we do, God stands ready to protect us. Psalm 147 promises, "He heals the brokenhearted and bandages their wounds" (v. 3, NCV).

When we are troubled, we must call upon God, and, in His own time and according to His own plan, He will heal us.

Are you anxious? Take those anxieties to God. Are you troubled? Take your troubles to Him. Does your world seem to be trembling beneath your feet? Seek protection from the One who cannot be moved. The same God who created the universe will protect you if you ask Him.

—·—·—·—·—·—·—

We all go through pain and sorrow, but the presence of God, like a warm, comforting blanket, can shield us and protect us, and allow the deep inner joy to surface, even in the most devastating circumstances.

Barbara Johnson

EARTHLY STRESS, HEAVENLY PEACE

Let the peace of Christ rule in your hearts, since as members of one body you were called to peace.

Colossians 3:15 NIV

Stressful days are an inevitable fact of modern life. And how do we best cope with the challenges of our demanding world? By turning our days and our lives over to God. Elisabeth Elliot writes, "If my life is surrendered to God, all is well. Let me not grab it back, as though it were in peril in His hand but would be safer in mine!" Yet even the most devout Christian woman may, at times, seek to grab the reins of her life and proclaim, "I'm in charge!" To do so is foolish, prideful, and stressful.

When we seek to impose our own wills upon the world we invite stress into our lives . . . needlessly. But, when we turn our lives and our hearts over to God and accept His will, we discover the inner peace that can be ours through Him.

Do you feel overwhelmed by the stresses of daily life? Turn your concerns and your prayers over to God. Trust Him completely. Trust Him always. When it comes to the inevitable challenges of this day, hand them over to God completely and without reservation. He knows your needs and will meet those needs in His own way and in His own time if you let Him.

FINDING PURPOSE THROUGH CHARITY

Happy is the person who thinks about the poor. When trouble comes, the Lord will save him.

Psalm 41:1 NCV

God's Words commands us to be generous, compassionate servants to those who need our support. As believers, we have been richly blessed by our Creator. We, in turn, are called to share our gifts, our possessions, our testimonies, and our talents.

Concentration camp survivor Corrie ten Boom correctly observed, "The measure of a life is not its duration but its donation." These words remind us that the quality of our lives is determined not by what we are able to take from others, but instead by what we are able to share with others.

The thread of generosity is woven into the very fabric of Christ's teachings. If we are to be His disciples, then we, too, must be cheerful, generous, courageous givers. Our Savior expects no less from us. And He deserves no less.

—·—·—·—·—·—·—·—

Generosity is changing one's focus from self to others.

John Maxwell

ACCORDING TO GOD

The counsel of the Lord stands forever, the plans of His heart from generation to generation.

Psalm 33:11 NASB

When you have a question that you simply can't answer, whom do you ask? When you face a difficult decision, to whom do you turn for counsel? To friends? To mentors? To family members? Or do you turn first to the Ultimate source of wisdom? The answers to life's Big Questions start with God and with the teachings of His Holy Word.

God's wisdom stands forever. God's Word is a light for every generation. Make it your light as well. Use the Bible as a compass for the next stage of your life's journey. Use it as the yardstick by which your behavior is measured. And as you carefully consult the pages of God's Word, prayerfully ask Him to reveal the wisdom that you need. When you take your concerns to God, He will not turn you away; He will, instead, offer answers that are tested and true. Your job is to ask, to listen, and to trust.

—.—.—.—.—.—.—.—

God Himself is what enlightens understanding about everything else in life. Knowledge about any subject is fragmentary without the enlightenment that comes from His relationship to it.

Beth Moore

PRAISE AND CRITICISM

Our only goal is to please God whether we live here or there, because we must all stand before Christ to be judged.

2 Corinthians 5:9-10 NCV

Rick Warren observed, "Those who follow the crowd usually get lost in it." We know those words to be true, but oftentimes we fail to live by them. Instead of trusting God for guidance, we imitate our friends and suffer the consequences. Instead of seeking to please our Father in heaven, we strive to please our peers, with decidedly mixed results. Instead of doing the right thing, we do the "easy" thing or the "popular" thing. And when we do, we pay a high price for our shortsightedness.

Would you like a time-tested formula for successful living? Here is a simple formula that is proven and true: don't give in to peer pressure. Period.

Instead of getting lost in the crowd, you should find guidance from God. Does this sound too simple? Perhaps it is simple, but it is also the only way to reap all the marvelous riches that God has in store for you.

—.—.—.—.—.—.—

Those who follow the crowd usually get lost in it.

Rick Warren

THE ULTIMATE PARTNER

For we are God's co-workers. You are God's field, God's building.

1 Corinthians 3:9 Holman CSB

If you want to be successful—genuinely successful in the things that really matter—you need a partner. That partner is God. And the good news is this: When you humbly and sincerely ask God to become your partner, He will grant your request and transform your life.

Is your life a testimony to the personal relationship that you enjoy with your Heavenly Father? Or have you compartmentalized your faith to a few hours on Sunday morning? If you genuinely wish to make God your fulltime partner, you must allow Him to reign over every aspect of your life and every day of your week. When you do, you'll be amazed at the things that the two of you, working together, can accomplish.

—.—.—.—.—.—.—.—

You can't climb the ladder of life with your hands in your pockets.

Barbara Johnson

GOD IS PERFECT; WE ARE NOT

Since we've compiled this long and sorry record as sinners (both us and them) and proved that we are utterly incapable of living the glorious lives God wills for us, God did it for us. Out of sheer generosity he put us in right standing with himself. A pure gift. He got us out of the mess we're in and restored us to where he always wanted us to be. And he did it by means of Jesus Christ.

Romans 3:23 MSG

Expectations, expectations, expectations! As a young woman living in the 21st century, you know that demands can be high, and expectations even higher. The media delivers an endless stream of messages that tell you how to look, how to behave, how to eat, and how to dress. The media's expectations are impossible to meet—God's are not. God doesn't expect you to be perfect . . . and neither should you.

Remember: the expectations that really matter are God's expectations. Everything else takes a back seat. So do your best to please God, and don't worry too much about what other people think. And, when it comes to meeting the unrealistic expectations of a world gone nuts, forget about trying to be perfect—it's impossible.

APART FROM THE WORLD

Don't love the world's ways. Don't love the world's goods. Love of the world squeezes out love for the Father. Practically everything that goes on in the world— wanting your own way, wanting everything for yourself, wanting to appear important—has nothing to do with the Father. It just isolates you from him. The world and all its wanting, wanting, wanting is on the way out—but whoever does what God wants is set for eternity.

1 John 2:15-17 MSG

All of mankind is engaged in a colossal, worldwide treasure hunt. Some people seek treasure from earthly sources, treasures such as material wealth or public acclaim; others seek God's treasures by making Him the cornerstone of their lives.

What kind of treasure hunter are you? Are you so caught up in the demands of everyday living that you sometimes allow the search for worldly treasures to become your primary focus? If so, it's time to reorganize your daily to-do list by placing God in His rightful place: first place. Don't allow anyone or anything to separate you from your Heavenly Father and His only begotten Son.

The world's treasures are difficult to find and difficult to keep; God's treasures are ever-present and everlasting. Which treasures, then, will you claim as your own?

A PERFECT TIMETABLE

He has made everything beautiful in its time.

Ecclesiastes 3:11 NIV

Are you anxious for God to work out His plan for your life? Who isn't? As believers, we all want God to do great things for us and through us, and we want Him to do those things now. But sometimes, God has other plans. Sometimes, God's timetable does not coincide with our own. It's worth noting, however, that God's timetable is always perfect.

The next time you find your patience tested to the limit, remember that the world unfolds according to God's plan, not ours. Sometimes, we must wait patiently, and that's as it should be. After all, think how patient God has been with us.

—··—··—··—··—

Waiting on God brings us to the journey's end quicker than our feet.

Mrs. Charles E. Cowman

GOD'S PERSPECTIVE

He will teach us His ways, and we shall walk in His paths.

Isaiah 2:3 NKJV

For most of us, life is busy and complicated. Amid the rush and crush of the daily grind, it is easy to lose perspective . . . easy, but wrong. When our world seems to be spinning out of control, we must simply seek to regain perspective by slowing ourselves down and then turning our thoughts and prayers toward God.

The familiar words of Psalm 46:10 remind us to "Be still, and know that I am God" (NKJV). When we do so, we encounter the awesome presence of our loving Heavenly Father, and we are blessed beyond words. But, when we ignore the presence of our Creator, we rob ourselves of His perspective, His peace, and His joy.

Today and every day, set aside a time to be still before God. When you do, you can face the day's complications with the wisdom and power that only He can provide.

—.—.—.—.—.—.—

When considering the size of your problems, there are two categories that you should never worry about: the problems that are small enough for you to handle, and the ones that aren't too big for God to handle.

Marie T. Freeman

HELPING TO BEAR THE BURDENS

Carry each other's burdens, and in this way you will fulfill the law of Christ.

Galatians 6:2 NIV

Neighbors. We know that we are instructed to love them, and yet there's so little time . . . and we're so busy. No matter. As Christians, we are commanded by our Lord and Savior Jesus Christ to love our neighbors just as we love ourselves. We are not asked to love our neighbors, nor are we encouraged to do so. We are commanded to love them. Period.

This very day, you will encounter someone who needs a word of encouragement or a pat on the back or a helping hand or a heartfelt prayer. And, if you don't reach out to that person, who will? If you don't take the time to understand the needs of your neighbors, who will? If you don't love your brothers and sisters, who will? So, today, look for a neighbor in need . . . and then do something to help. Father's orders.

—·—·—·—·—·—·—

Love is an attribute of God. To love others is evidence of a genuine faith.

Kay Arthur

GOD'S STRENGTH FOR THE DAY AHEAD

*My God is my rock, in whom I take refuge, my shield
and the horn of my salvation.*

2 Samuel 22:2-3 NIV

God is a never-ending source of support and
courage for those of us who call upon Him. When we
are weary, He gives us strength. When we see no hope,
God reminds us of His promises. When we grieve, God
wipes away our tears.

Do the demands of this day threaten to overwhelm
you? If so, you must rely not only upon your own resources, but also upon the promises of your Father in heaven.
God will hold your hand and walk with you every day of
your life if you let Him. So even if your circumstances are
difficult, trust the Father. His love is eternal and His goodness endures forever.

—.—.—.—.—.—.—

In God's faithfulness lies eternal security.

Corrie ten Boom

WALKING THE CHRISTIAN PATH

And don't be wishing you were someplace else or with someone else. Where you are right now is God's place for you. Live and obey and love and believe right there.

1 Corinthians 7:17 MSG

Each day, as we awaken from sleep, we are confronted with countless opportunities to serve God and to follow in the footsteps of His Son. When we do, our Heavenly Father guides our steps and blesses our endeavors.

As citizens of a fast-changing world, we face challenges that sometimes leave us feeling overworked, over-committed, and overwhelmed. But God has different plans for us. He intends that we slow down long enough to praise Him and to glorify His Son. When we do, He lifts our spirits and enriches our lives.

Today provides a glorious opportunity to place yourself in the service of the One who is the Giver of all blessings. May you seek His will, may you trust His word, and may you walk in the footsteps of His Son.

—.—.—.—.—.—.—

Life is immortal, love eternal; death is nothing but a horizon, and a horizon is only the limit of our vision.

Corrie ten Boom

PRAISE FOR THE FATHER; THANKS FOR HIS BLESSINGS

I will give You thanks with all my heart.

Psalm 138:1 Holman CSB

If you're like most folks on the planet, you're a very busy person. Your life is probably hectic, demanding, and complicated. And when the demands of life leave you rushing from place to place with scarcely a moment to spare, you may not take time to praise your Creator. Big mistake.

The Bible makes it clear: it pays to praise God. Worship and praise should be a part of everything you do. Otherwise, you quickly lose perspective as you fall prey to the demands of everyday life.

Do you sincerely desire to know God in a more meaningful way? Then praise Him for who He is and for what He has done for you. And please don't wait until Sunday morning—praise Him all day long, every day, for as long as you live . . . and then for all eternity.

—.—.—.—.—.—.—

The time for universal praise is sure to come some day. Let us begin to do our part now.

Hannah Whitall Smith

PRAYING TO KNOW GOD

Teach me your ways, O Lord, that I may live according to your truth! Grant me purity of heart, that I may honor you.

Psalm 86:11 NLT

Andrew Murray observed, "Some people pray just to pray, and some people pray to know God." Your task, as a maturing believer, is to pray, not out of habit or obligation, but out of a sincere desire to know your Heavenly Father. Through constant prayers, you should petition God, you should praise Him, and you should seek to discover His unfolding plans for your life.

Today, reach out to the Giver of all blessings. Turn to Him for guidance and for strength. Invite Him into every corner of your day. Ask Him to teach you and to lead you. And remember that no matter what your circumstances, God is never far away; He is here . . . always right here. So pray.

—.—.—.—.—.—.—

We rarely discover anything monumental about God without discovering something momentous about ourselves. With every revelation comes an invitation to adjust out lives to what we have seen.

Beth Moore

THE COURAGE TO RISK FAILURE

The fear of human opinion disables; trusting in God protects you from that.

Proverbs 29:25 MSG

As we consider the uncertainties of the future, we are confronted with a powerful temptation: the temptation to "play it safe." Unwilling to move mountains, we fret over molehills. Unwilling to entertain great hopes for tomorrow, we focus on the unfairness of today. Unwilling to trust God completely, we take timid half-steps when God intends that we make giant leaps.

Today, ask God for the courage to step beyond the boundaries of your doubts. Ask Him to guide you to a place where you can realize your full potential—a place where you are freed from the fear of failure. Ask Him to do His part, and promise Him that you will do your part. Don't ask Him to lead you to a "safe" place; ask Him to lead you to the "right" place . . . and remember: those two places are seldom the same.

—.—.—.—.—.—.—

How beautiful it is to learn that grace isn't fragile, and that in the family of God we can fail and not be a failure.

Gloria Gaither

WHEN HIS PEACE BECOMES OUR PEACE

But now in Christ Jesus you who formerly were far off have been brought near by the blood of Christ. For He Himself is our peace.

Ephesians 2:13-14 NASB

Have you found the genuine peace that can be yours through Jesus Christ? Or are you still rushing after the illusion of "peace and happiness" that the world promises but cannot deliver?

The beautiful words of John 14:27 remind us that Jesus offers us peace, not as the world gives, but as He alone gives: "Peace I leave with you, My peace I give to you; not as the world gives do I give to you. Let not your heart be troubled, neither let it be afraid" (NKJV). Our challenge is to accept Christ's peace and then, as best we can, to share His blessings with our neighbors.

Today, as a gift to yourself, to your family, and to the world, let Christ's peace become your peace. Let Him rule your heart and your thoughts. When you do, you will partake in the peace that only He can give.

—·—·—·—·—·—·—

We must learn to move according to the timetable of the Timeless One, and to be at peace.

Elisabeth Elliot

SEARCHING FOR THE RIGHT KIND OF TREASURE

Wherever your treasure is, there your heart and thoughts will also be.

Luke 12:34 NLT

Is God a big priority for you . . . or is He an afterthought? Do you give God your best or what's left? Have you given Christ your heart, your soul, your talents, your time, and your testimony? Or are you giving Him little more than a few hours each Sunday morning?

In the book of Exodus, God warns that we should place no gods before Him (Exodus 20:3). Yet all too often, we place our Lord in second, third, or fourth place as we worship the gods of pride, money, or personal gratification. When we unwittingly place possessions or relationships above our love for the Creator, we must realign our priorities or suffer the consequences.

Does God rule your heart? Make certain that the honest answer to this question is a resounding yes. In the life of every radical believer, God comes first. And that's precisely the place that He deserves in your heart.

—.—.—.—.—.—.—

The things that matter most in this world can never be held in your hand.

Gloria Gaither

STANDING ON THE ROCK

Anyone who listens to my teaching and obeys me is wise, like a person who builds a house on solid rock. Though the rain comes in torrents and the floodwaters rise and the winds beat against that house, it won't collapse, because it is built on rock.

Matthew 7:24-25 NLT

God is the Creator of life, the Sustainer of life, and the Rock upon which righteous lives are built. God is a never-ending source of support for those who trust Him, and He is a never-ending source of wisdom for those who study His Holy Word.

Is God the Rock upon which you've constructed your own life? If so, then you have chosen wisely. Your faith will give you the inner strength you need to rise above the inevitable demands and struggles of life-here-on-earth.

Do the demands of this day seem overwhelming? If so, you must rely not only upon your own resources, but more importantly upon the Rock that cannot be shaken. God will hold your hand and walk with you today and every day if you let Him. Even if your circumstances are difficult, trust the Father. His promises remain true; His love is eternal; and His goodness endures. And because He is the One who can never be moved, you can stand firm in the knowledge that you are protected by Him now and forever.

STEERING CLEAR OF THE ROAD TO RUIN

Innocent people will be kept safe, but those who are dishonest will suddenly be ruined.

Proverbs 28:18 NCV

How hard is it to bump into temptation in this crazy world? Not very hard. The devil, it seems, is causing pain and heartache in more places and in more ways than ever before. We, as Christians, must remain vigilant. Not only must we resist Satan when he confronts us, but we must also avoid those places where Satan can most easily tempt us. And, if we are to avoid the unending temptations of this world, we must earnestly wrap ourselves in the protection of God's Holy Word.

The road to ruin is wide, long, and deadly. Avoid it, and help others do the same. When you do, God will smile—and the devil won't.

—.—.—.—.—.—.—

When a person comes to God, just as she is—while still in her sinning state—God looks at her and because of what Jesus Christ did on the cross he proclaims her righteous.

Luci Swindoll

FROM THE INSIDE OUT

No one will say, "Look here!" or "There!" For you see, the kingdom of God is among you.

Luke 17:21 Holman CSB

If we sincerely want to change ourselves for the better, we must start on the inside and work our way out from there. Lasting change doesn't occur "out there"; it occurs "in here." It occurs, not in the shifting sands of our own particular circumstances, but in the quiet depths of our own hearts.

Do you desire to improve some aspect of your life? If so, don't expect changing circumstances to miraculously transform you into the person you want to become. Transformation starts with God, and it starts in the silent center of a humble human heart—like yours.

—.—.—.—.—.—.—

Conditions are always changing; therefore, I must not be dependent upon conditions. What matters supremely is my soul and my relationship to God.

Corrie ten Boom

LEARNING FROM THE FAITHFUL

We have around us many people whose lives tell us what faith means. So let us run the race that is before us and never give up. We should remove from our lives anything that would get in the way and the sin that so easily holds us back.

Hebrews 12:1 NCV

It has been said on many occasions that life is a team sport. So, too, is learning how to live. If we are to become mature believers—and if we seek to discover God's purposes in our everyday lives—we need worthy examples and wise mentors.

Are you walking with the wise? Are you spending time with people you admire? Are you learning how to live from people who know how to live? If you genuinely seek to walk with God, then you will walk with those who walk with Him.

—·—·—·—·—·—

Recently I've been learning that life comes down to this: God is in everything. Regardless of what difficulties I am experiencing at the moment, or what things aren't as I would like them to be, I look at the circumstances and say, "Lord, what are you trying to teach me?"

Catherine Marshall

IN SEARCH OF ANSWERS

You will seek me and find me when you seek me with all your heart.

Jeremiah 29:13 NIV

You've got questions? God's got answers. And if you'd like to hear from Him, here's precisely what you must do: petition Him with a sincere heart; be still; be patient; and listen. Then, in His own time and in His own fashion, God will answer your questions and give you guidance for the journey ahead.

Today, turn over everything to your Creator. Pray constantly about matters great and small. Seek God's instruction and His direction. And remember: God hears your prayers and answers them. But He won't answer the prayers that you don't get around to praying. So pray early and often. And then wait patiently for answers that are sure to come.

—.—.—.—.—.—.—

The purpose of all prayer is to find God's will and to make that will our prayer.

Catherine Marshall

SERVING GOD WITH HUMILITY

Jesus sat down and called the twelve apostles to him. He said, "Whoever wants to be the most important must be last of all and servant of all."

Mark 9:35 NCV

The teachings of Jesus are clear: We achieve greatness through service to others. But, as weak human beings, we sometimes fall short as we seek to puff ourselves up and glorify our own accomplishments. Jesus commands otherwise. He teaches us that the most esteemed men and women are not the self-congratulatory leaders of society but are instead the humblest of servants.

Today, you may feel the temptation to build yourself up in the eyes of your neighbors. Resist that temptation. Instead, serve your neighbors quietly and without fanfare. Find a need and fill it . . . humbly. Lend a helping hand and share a word of kindness . . . anonymously, for this is God's way.

As a humble servant, you will glorify yourself not before people, but before God, and that's what God intends. After all, earthly glory is fleeting: here today and all too soon gone. But, heavenly glory endures throughout eternity. So, the choice is yours: Either you can lift yourself up here on earth and be humbled in heaven, or vice versa. Choose vice versa.

DISCERNING SPIRITUAL TRUTHS

A person who does not have the Spirit does not accept the truths that come from the Spirit of God. That person thinks they are foolish and cannot understand them, because they can only be judged to be true by the Spirit. The spiritual person is able to judge all things, but no one can judge him.

1 Corinthians 2:14–15 NCV

When God's Sspirit touches our hearts, we are confronted by a powerful force: the awesome, irresistible force of God's Truth. In response to that force, we will either follow God's lead by allowing Him to guide our thoughts and deeds, or we will resist God's calling and accept the consequences of our rebellion.

Today, as you fulfill the responsibilities that God has placed before you, ask yourself this question: "Do my thoughts and actions bear witness to the ultimate Truth that God has placed in my heart, or am I allowing the pressures of everyday life to overwhelm me?" It's a profound question that only you can answer. You be the judge.

—.—.—.—.—.—.—

As we spend time reading, applying, and obeying our Bibles, the Spirit of Truth who is also the Spirit of Jesus increasingly reveals Jesus to us.

Anne Graham Lotz

HAPPY TOMORROW

Whereas you do not know what will happen tomorrow.
For what is your life? It is even a vapor that appears for
a little time and then vanishes away.

James 4:14 NJKV

Life should never be taken for granted. Each day is a priceless gift from God and should be treated as such.

Hannah Whitall Smith observed, "How changed our lives would be if we could only fly through the days on wings of surrender and trust!" And Clement of Alexandria noted, "All our life is a celebration for us; we are convinced, in fact, that God is always everywhere. We sing while we work . . . we pray while we carry out all life's other occupations." These words remind us that this day is God's creation, a gift to be treasured and savored.

Today, let us celebrate life with smiles on our faces and kind words on our lips. After all, this is God's day, and He has given us clear instructions for its use. We are commanded to rejoice and be glad. So, with no further ado, let the celebration begin . . .

—.—.—.—.—.—.—.—

When your life comes to a close, you will remember not days but moments. Treasure each one.

Barbara Johnson

BUSY WITH OUR THOUGHTS

So prepare your minds for service and have self-control.

1 Peter 1:13 NCV

Because we are human, we are always busy with our thoughts. We simply can't help ourselves. Our brains never shut off, and even while we're sleeping, we mull things over in our minds. The question is not if we will think; the question is how will we think and what will we think about.

Today, focus your thoughts on God and His will. And if you've been plagued by pessimism and doubt, stop thinking like that! Place your faith in God and give thanks for His blessings. Think optimistically about your world and your life. It's the wise way to use your mind. And besides, since you will always be busy with your thoughts, you might as well make those thoughts pleasing (to God) and helpful (to you and yours).

—.—.—.—.—.—.—

No matter how little we can change about our circumstances, we always have a choice about our attitude toward the situation.

Vonette Bright

COMPASSION AND COURTESY IN A DISCOURTEOUS WORLD

Finally, all of you should be of one mind, full of sympathy toward each other, loving one another with tender hearts and humble minds.

1 Peter 3:8 NLT

As Christians, we are instructed to be courteous and compassionate. As believers, we are called to be gracious, humble, gentle, and kind. But sometimes, we fall short. Sometimes, amid the busyness and confusion of everyday life, we may neglect to share a kind word or a kind deed. This oversight hurts others, and it hurts us as well.

Today, slow yourself down and be alert for those who need your smile, your kind words, or your helping hand. Make kindness a centerpiece of your dealings with others. They will be blessed, and you will be, too. So make this promise to yourself and keep it: honor Christ by obeying His Golden Rule. He deserves no less. And neither, for that matter, do they.

—.—.—.—.—.—.—

It doesn't take monumental feats to make the world a better place. It can be as simple as letting someone go ahead of you in a grocery line.

Barbara Johnson

WHOM WE SHOULD JUDGE

Stop judging others, and you will not be judged. Stop criticizing others, or it will all come back on you. If you forgive others, you will be forgiven.

Luke 6:37 NLT

The warning of Matthew 7:1 is clear: "Judge not, that ye be not judged" (KJV). Yet even the most devoted Christians may fall prey to a powerful yet subtle temptation: the temptation to judge others. But as obedient followers of Christ, we are commanded to refrain from such behavior.

As Jesus came upon a young woman who had been condemned by the Pharisees, He spoke not only to the crowd that was gathered there, but also to all generations when He warned, "He that is without sin among you, let him first cast a stone at her" (John 8:7 KJV). Christ's message is clear, and it applies not only to the Pharisees of ancient times, but also to us.

—.—.—.—.—.—.—.—

Don't judge other people more harshly than you want God to judge you.

Marie T. Freeman

WISDOM FROM THE HEART

But what happens when we live God's way? He brings gifts into our lives, much the same way that fruit appears in an orchard—things like affection for others, exuberance about life, serenity. We develop a willingness to stick with things, a sense of compassion in the heart, and a conviction that a basic holiness permeates things and people. We find ourselves involved in loyal commitments, not needing to force our way in life, able to marshal and direct our energies wisely. Legalism is helpless in bringing this about; it only gets in the way.

Galatians 5:22-23 MSG

When we genuinely open our hearts to God, He speaks to us through a small, still voice within. When He does, we can listen, or not. When we pay careful attention to the Father, He leads us along a path of His choosing, a path that leads to abundance, peace, joy, and eternal life. But when we choose to ignore God, we select a path that is not His, and we must endure the consequences of our shortsightedness.

Today, focus your thoughts and your prayers on the path that God intends for you to take. When you do, your loving Heavenly Father will speak to your heart. When He does, listen carefully . . . and trust Him.

THINK NOW, ACT LATER

Enthusiasm without knowledge is not good. If you act too quickly, you might make a mistake.

Proverbs 19:2 NCV

Are you, at times, just a little bit impulsive? Do you sometimes fail to look before you leap? If so, God wants to have a little chat with you.

God's Word is clear: as believers, we are called to lead lives of discipline, diligence, moderation, and maturity. But the world often tempts us to behave otherwise. Everywhere we turn, or so it seems, we are faced with powerful temptations to behave in undisciplined, ungodly ways.

God's Word instructs us to be disciplined in our thoughts and our actions; God's Word warns us against the dangers of impulsive behavior. As believers in a just God, we should act and react accordingly.

—.—.—.—.—.—.—

I do not know how the Spirit of Christ performs it, but He brings us choices through which we constantly change, fresh and new, into His likeness.

Joni Eareckson Tada

THE RICHES OF HIS GRACE

In him we have redemption through his blood, the forgiveness of sins, in accordance with the riches of God's grace that he lavished on us with all wisdom and understanding.

Ephesians 1:7-8 NIV

We are saved, not by our own righteousness, but by God's grace. God's priceless gift of eternal life is not a reward for our good deeds; it is a manifestation of God's infinite love for those who worship Him and accept His Son as their Savior.

Are you absolutely certain that you have accepted the gift of salvation? If not, drop to your knees this very instant and accept Christ as your personal Savior. And, if you are already the thankful recipient of eternal life through Christ Jesus, use this day as an opportunity to share your testimony with friends and family members.

Jesus is the sovereign Friend and ultimate Savior of mankind. Christ showed enduring love for us by willingly sacrificing His own life so that we might have eternal life. Let us love Him, praise Him, and share His message of salvation with our neighbors and with the world.

—.—.—.—.—.—.—

God's grace and power seem to reach their peak when we are at our weakest point.

Anne Graham Lo

PROBLEM-SOLVING 101

*People who do what is right may have many problems,
but the Lord will solve them all.*

Psalm 34:19 NCV

Life is an exercise in problem-solving. The question is not whether we will encounter problems; the real question is how we will choose to address them. When it comes to solving the problems of everyday living, we often know precisely what needs to be done, but we may be slow in doing it—especially if what needs to be done is difficult or uncomfortable for us. So we put off till tomorrow what should be done today.

The words of Psalm 34 remind us that the Lord solves problems for "people who do what is right." And usually, doing "what is right" means doing the uncomfortable work of confronting our problems sooner rather than later. So with no further ado, let the problem-solving begin . . . now.

—·—·—·—·—·—·—

Life is simply hard. That's all there is to it. Thank goodness, the intensity of difficulty rises and falls. Some seasons are far more bearable than others but none is without challenge.

Beth Moore

YOUR SHINING LIGHT

You are the light of the world. A city on a hill cannot be hidden. Neither do people light a lamp and put it under a bowl. Instead they put it on its stand, and it gives light to everyone in the house. In the same way, let your light shine before men, that they may see your good deeds and praise your Father in heaven.

Matthew 5:14-16 NIV

Whether we like it or not, we are role models. Hopefully, the lives we lead and the choices we make will serve as enduring examples of the spiritual abundance that is available to all who worship God and obey His commandments.

Ask yourself this question: Are you the kind of role model that you would want to emulate? If so, congratulations. But if certain aspects of your behavior could stand improvement, the best day to begin your self-improvement regimen is this one. Because whether you realize it or not, people you love are watching your behavior, and they're learning how to live. You owe it to them—and to yourself—to live righteously and well.

—·—·—·—·—·—·—

In your desire to share the gospel, you may be the only Jesus someone else will ever meet. Be real and be involved with people.

Barbara Johnso

GOD'S PERFECT LOVE

This is what real love is: It is not our love for God; it is God's love for us in sending his Son to be the way to take away our sins.

1 John 4:10 NCV

St. Augustine observed, "God loves each of us as if there were only one of us." Do you believe those words? Do you seek to have an intimate, one-on-one relationship with your Heavenly Father, or are you satisfied to keep Him at a "safe" distance?

Sometimes, in the crush of our daily duties, God may seem far away, but He is not. God is everywhere we have ever been and everywhere we will ever go. He is with us night and day; He knows our thoughts and our prayers. And, when we earnestly seek Him, we will find Him because He is here, waiting patiently for us to reach out to Him.

Let us reach out to Him today and always. And let us praise Him for the glorious gifts that have transformed us today and forever. Amen.

—·—·—·—·—·—

God is a God of unconditional, unremitting love, a love that corrects and chastens but never ceases.

Kay Arthur

SUCCESS ACCORDING TO GOD

Live the way the Lord your God has commanded you so that you may live and have what is good.

Deuteronomy 5:33 NCV

How do you define success? Do you define it as the accumulation of material possessions or the adulation of your friends? If so, you need to reorder your priorities. Genuine success has little to do with fame or fortune; it has everything to do with God's gift of love and with His promise of salvation.

If you have allowed Christ to reign over your life, you are already a towering success in the eyes of God, but there is still more that you can do. Your task—as a believer who has been touched by the Creator's grace—is to accept the spiritual abundance and peace that He offers through the person of His Son. Then, you can share the healing message of God's love and His abundance with a world that desperately needs both. When you do, you have reached the pinnacle of success.

—·—·—·—·—·—·—

Success isn't the key. Faithfulness is.

Joni Eareckson Tada

NEW AND IMPROVED

Your old life is dead. Your new life, which is your real life—even though invisible to spectators—is with Christ in God. He is your life.

Colossians 3:3 MSG

Has your relationship with Jesus transformed you into an extremely different person? Hopefully so! Otherwise, you're missing out on the joy and abundance that can be yours through Christ.

Think, for a moment, about the "old" you, the person you were before you invited Christ to reign over your heart. Now, think about the "new" you, the person you've become since then. Is there a difference between the "old" version of you and the "new-and-improved" version? There should be! And that difference should be evident to you, to your family, and to your friends.

When you invited Christ to reign over your heart, you became a radically new creation. This day offers yet another opportunity to behave yourself like that new person. When you do, God will guide your steps and bless your endeavors . . . forever.

Are you willing to make radical changes for Jesus? If so, you may be certain of this fact: He's standing at the door of your heart, patiently waiting to form an extreme, life-altering relationship with you.

GOD IS LOVE

We know how much God loves us, and we have put our trust in him. God is love, and all who live in love live in God, and God lives in them.

1 John 4:16 NLT

God's love for you is deeper and more profound than you can fathom. And now, precisely because you are a wondrous creation treasured by God, a question presents itself: What will you do in response to God's love? Will you ignore it or embrace it? Will you return it or neglect it? The decision, of course, is yours and yours alone.

When you embrace God's love, you are forever changed. When you embrace God's love, you feel differently about yourself, your neighbors, and your world. When you embrace God's love, you share His message and you obey His commandments.

When you accept the Father's grace and share His love, you are blessed here on earth and throughout all eternity. Accept His love today.

—.—.—.—.—.—.—

The essence of God's being is love—He never separates Himself from that.

Kay Arthur

MEMORIES FROM THIS YEAR

MEMORIES

MEMORIES

MEMORIES

MEMORIES

MEMORIES

MEMORIES

MEMORIES

MEMORIES

MEMORIES